Peace be with you

Dillon Cruz

Go Golden

Go Golden

Applying a Universal Religious Teaching and the Ethics of
Permaculture to Create a Sustainable, Just, Happier Society

DILLON NABER CRUZ

Foreword by Lee C. Barrett

RESOURCE *Publications* • Eugene, Oregon

GO GOLDEN
Applying a Universal Religious Teaching and the Ethics of Permaculture to Create a
Sustainable, Just, Happier Society

Resource Publications
An Imprint of Wipf and Stock Publishers
199 W. 8th Ave., Suite 3
Eugene, OR 97401

www.wipfandstock.com

PAPERBACK ISBN: 978-1-5326-6204-1
HARDCOVER ISBN: 978-1-5326-6205-8
EBOOK ISBN: 978-1-5326-6206-5

Manufactured in the U.S.A.   NOVEMBER 6, 2018

For Harli Michelle and Whitney Rae

Contents

Foreword

As Dillon Cruz warns, our fragile planet is like the Titanic headed for an iceberg, only now there are no life boats at all and no place of refuge. With passion and eloquence Cruz communicates the sense of urgency that all citizens of the earth should feel in the face of the looming ecological catastrophe. This book is a strident alarm bell; it is loud, jolting, and insistent, but it is also absolutely imperative that this alarm awaken us from our comfortable slumbers.

Cruz is not a prophet of inevitable doom; he does not leave the reader forlorn and hopeless. As he notes, the planetary crisis has been created by human beings, and it can still be reversed by human beings. What humans have foolishly done, they can undo. Using the principles of permaculture design, Cruz sketches a way forward toward global survival and sustainability.

The value of employing permaculture theory to develop a vision for the future is its holistic approach to understanding the basic dynamics of any environment, big or small. Permaculture views phenomena as intersections of complex factors, none of which should be treated in isolation from the others. The big picture must be taken into account, even in the design of a garden. Consequently, Cruz attends to food production, the consumption of goods, domestic dwellings, national politics, and international relations. All of these factors interact with one another in complex ways to generate our current desperate predicament. For example, our patterns of food consumption cannot be understood or addressed without seeing how they are entangled in our cultural habits of thoughtless consumerism and in nationalistic political ambitions. Dealing with just one of these factors without attending to the others would yield only negligible results.

Cruz implicitly advances two powerful arguments to support his permaculture approach. One is that it is in everyone's self-interest to do so. If we fail to confront the planetary crisis in a holistic manner, we have condemned ourselves and our species to extinction. No one in their right mind would want to struggle to eke out a minimal existence on a pile of inert dirt, even if such a futile struggle were remotely possible.

Secondly, Cruz appeals throughout to the ethical imperative to do unto others as you would have them do unto you. The power of this principle seems to be hard-wired into human beings, for it emerges and reemerges in all major religious and ideological traditions. Appealing to the Golden Rule, Cruz expands the scope of "others" to include all sentient beings, and, in fact, all entities. For example, the deplorable plight of milk cows suffering from grotesquely enlarged udders and hoof disease is exposed with brutal candor, and the expectation is that only those who are irredeemably callous would tolerate such misery in another life-form. The book is a call to look deep into ourselves and find untapped reservoirs of empathy for all creatures.

Like all prophetic words, this volume is a call to repentance and change. Our problem is not just pragmatic or technical; it is at its core a cultural, spiritual, and ideological issue. We humans must learn to see the world differently and modify our behavior accordingly. We must learn to become less greedy, less myopic, less tribal, and less concerned with short-term benefits. Most importantly, we must resolve to become less selfish. That is a tall order, but the alternative is dreadful.

LEE C. BARRETT
Stager Professor of Theology, Lancaster Theological Seminary

Preface

THIS BOOK IS BOTH a culmination and a stopping point on my personal theological and permaculture journey. These days, theology and permaculture are so entwined for me that I can scarcely separate them. The groundwork for this book began many years ago, before I realized that I was thinking about matters related to God's creation and humanity's treatment of it from a theological perspective. In a conversation with Episcopal Bishop, and former Dean of the National Cathedral. Rev. Dr. Nathan Baxter, about permaculture in 2018, he mentioned that from what I had told him about permaculture and my spiritual journey, that he could see that I had indeed been thinking theologically about the care of creation since my time in the Marine Corps back in the early 1990s. The tendency towards thinking theologically about everyday life continues to grow in me and likely will for quite some time.

The Christianity I grew up with and stayed with into my early thirties had little to no time for God's creation. It was instead focused on what I now call "sin management," personal salvation, and the eternal destination of one's individual soul. Theologically speaking, it was, and remains, an incredibly self-centered, otherworldly, and judgmental way of thinking about God and our Earthly existence. From my perspective, it often missed major points of emphasis from Jesus' life and ministry. It saw creation as a thing to be not only subdued, but exploited to the point of destruction. This made no sense to me as someone, who taking my cue from the Book of Genesis, saw God's beautiful creation as good.

I left the church in 2003 feeling disillusioned, angry, and more than a little traumatized. By 2015, I was feeling spiritually adrift, alone, and without purpose. In a conversation with my oldest friend Jeff Mahan, a man I've known since we were in the sixth grade, he told me that he would prayerfully consider my existential and spiritual conundrum. As he has been endowed with the gift of discernment, I waited anxiously to learn if the Holy Spirit had given him any guidance on my behalf. When he told me that the Holy Spirit had led him to the conclusion that I was called to tell Christian America about ecological stewardship and permaculture, I was incredulous because I had not been a member of, or even an occasional visitor to a Christian church in over twelve years. God's ways not being our ways however, and being mysterious as well, Jeff's discernment turned out to be spot on and my incredulity was made to look foolish with the benefit of hindsight.

Things moved with great rapidity from that point on in 2015. I suddenly found myself talking to the admissions office at Lancaster Theological Seminary (LTS) and reading books about Jesus. Not long after that initial conversation at LTS' admissions office, in which I said everything I could to persuade the Director of Vocations that I didn't belong there, I read a line in a book that a friend had loaned me entitled *The Jesus Driven Life: Reconnecting Humanity with Jesus* by theologian and scholar of mimetic theory, Michael Hardin, that in essence said that by following the spiritual path of Jesus, humanity could bring healing to the world. As I read the paragraph that that sentence is found in, I became overwhelmed with emotion and had one of those numinous experiences where one gets goose pumps everywhere. As the tears rolled down my face, I knew that I was going to seminary. Shortly thereafter, I found a wonderful church home where I have been a member for the past couple of years.

While at LTS, it became clear that I was not called to be a pastor. My vocation lies outside the pulpit, so I changed programs to an academic Master's degree and started writing my thesis, which has since become the manuscript for this book. My previous studies of permaculture design, as well as lived experience in practicing permaculture in a variety of capacities blended with near perfection with my academic study of theology at LTS. The result is this book. Permaculture and theology challenge me on a daily basis to learn how to better live in harmony with the Earth and my neighbors. Writing this book has challenged me further to live in accordance with my ethics and theological beliefs. I have a long way to go. I hope this book inspires readers to develop a deeper commitment to ecological stewardship, regeneration, and the spiritual practice of loving your neighbors. The Golden Rule is so simple, so elegant, and so important. May we all learn to live it out each day.

Peace be with you.

DILLON NABER CRUZ
Lancaster, PA
October 2018

Acknowledgments

WRITING A BOOK IS a huge task that is so much more than getting ideas onto the page in a reasonably coherent and interesting manner. This being my first book, I had no idea just how much work goes into the process of researching, compiling, writing, revising, editing, rewriting, formatting, and copyediting a manuscript before it becomes an actual book. Much of what had to be done was beyond my skills set, and many pairs of eyes have seen the various incarnations of the following chapters. All of this to say, I could not have written this book alone and there are many people to thank who helped me get this done.

Educators are high on the list for my gratitude, for without them, not one word of this book gets written. Undergraduate professors Kurt Depner and Pat Aguilar (El Paso Community College); Dan Furst (Leeward Community College); Erin Shelor, Clarence Maxwell, and John McClarnon (Millersville University) all challenged me to hone my craft as a researcher and writer. The entire faculty of Lancaster Theological Seminary, about whom I could gush effusively, deepened my knowledge, helped me further hone my craft as a writer, and encouraged me throughout my seminary studies. Dr. Lee Barrett, my advisor and theology professor, opened up the world of theology to me and kindled a latent ember into a flame of intellectual and spiritual curiosity that will burn throughout my life. He also acted as my thesis advisor and that thesis evolved into this book.

David Mellott, Julia O'Brien, Greg Carey, Ann Thayer, and Stephanie Crumpton, LTS faculty during my two years there, all shaped my knowledge, generated enthusiasm for scholarship, and helped me to get past the impostor syndrome I often felt in seminary. Erika Fitz and Bishop Nathan Baxter, adjunct professors at LTS, both spent significant time with me during my classes with them allowing me to formulate ideas and integrate learning in ways that indirectly shaped this book.

A special mention too must go to the teachers, practitioners, and visionaries of the permaculture community that I have been privileged to meet, learn from, and work with. They are: Albert Bates, Cliff and Jennifer Davis, Jennifer Morgan, Matthew English, Andrew Millison, Jude Hobbs, Dash and Erika Kuhr, Dave Jacke, Scott Mann, Ben Weiss, Wilson Alvarez, Jono Droege, and Donna Volles. Thank you all for your all you do for our planet and for all the ways you've taught and inspired me on my journey.

I'm pretty good at writing interesting sentences. I'm not so good at details like formatting, punctuation, and getting all of the proverbial I's and T's both dotted and crossed. Frank Gray, the wizard of the LTS writing center, and Heidi Seibels, my friend and editor extraordinaire, are both excellent at all of those things. Frank read every word of my thesis and made many helpful suggestions as well as pointing out grammatical errors that I missed. Heidi has walked me through the revising, editing and formatting process with patience and expertise. It is no understatement to say that this book does not happen without her input.

Lastly, and certainly not least, my family and friends who have loved me unconditionally and encouraged me so often, my gratitude knows no bounds. I love you all.

How to Read This Book

EACH OF THE FOLLOWING chapters is on a distinct subject. Similar to the permaculture concept of zones, the chapters proceed from Zone 0 (our own bodies) by talking about the foods we eat and the processes by which that food is produced in Chapter 1, and then move outward away from our physical bodies to zones farther away in Chapter 2. Chapter 3 is about our cultural patterns of consumption which correlates to Zone One (see chapter 7) while Chapter 4 is about our homes (Zone 2). Chapters 5 and 6 take us farther away from ourselves and into Zones 3 and 4, with Chapter 5 dealing with our national politics, and Chapter 6 with issues of war and peace. Chapter 7 is an introduction to permaculture design which will include a detailed description of the permaculture zones, principles, and ethics as well as further details about the need for such a design system. The chapters can be read in any order, but the reader may find it most useful to read them in the order presented.

1.

Go Golden

An Introduction

MUCH HAS BEEN WRITTEN by people, ranging from scientists to advertisers, about the importance of people "Going Green" to stave off the effects of global climate change, the potentials of which are downright scary, and to conserve the ever-dwindling supplies of fossil fuels as well as other natural resources that all life depends upon. Oftentimes a marketing department's or advertiser's idea of "Going Green" is little more than an intentional attempt to deceive their customers into buying something that is only slightly less harmful to the environment than their other products or an attempt to stand out from their competition. Others use these techniques simply as a way to justify consumerism of a different type, convincing customers that they can still shop all that they want to and be guilt free. At other times, it is simply "Green Washing," using verbiage, packaging, and other marketing tricks meant to fool the buyer into buying a product that is anything but "Green."

There is no doubt in my mind that the overwhelming majority of scientists who are giving us their dire warnings about the ecological health of this planet's biosphere are absolutely correct.[1] The Good Ship Earth is indeed sailing towards a proverbial iceberg capable of bringing it and its human passengers down like the Titanic, only without the benefit of lifeboats. There is no Planet B. Scientists have been warning political leaders[2] and the general public that sea levels will rise and extreme weather events

1. NASA, "Scientific Consensus."
2. Risen, "Scientists Warn Congress."

such as prolonged droughts, more frequent wildfires, excessive heat or cold, increased numbers and more intense hurricanes, tornado outbreaks, and monsoon-like rainfall events that cause widespread flooding,[3] will become much more prevalent and will negatively affect agricultural yields, subsume small island nations, and make other countries nearly uninhabitable due to extreme heat or cold. Yet there are things that can and *must* be done to reverse the course of our planetary ship, which is being captained by an ostensibly intelligent and reasonably sane humanity, if we but apply ourselves to solving the problems with the alacrity that the magnitude that the climate change issues warrant. Each of us as individuals, particularly those of us in wealthy nations, can start by seeing the ways in which our actions affect people both near to us and those across the oceans. It is our actions which determine our treatment of people whether they live near to us or far away.

Imagine a world where The Golden Rule was applied as a matter of course in all aspects of life, where every decision we as individuals and as a society was run through the rubric of the Golden Rule before it was made and implemented. How remarkably different the planet would look and feel for billions of people and other forms of life, many of which humanity counts on for survival. I believe that nearly, if not all, aspects of modern life would be changed for the better if we collectively agreed to this principle and then took such an action. I hope to elucidate just such a vision within these pages, and by so doing, bring forth some light into previously dark places. As a culturally Christian person on a journey to know the Creator through the teachings of a well-known Galilean shaman[4], I want to more fully become this change, live this change, and inspire this change that I wish to see in the world.

There is a certain amount of back story, personal, geopolitical, historical, and ecological that must needs be presented in order to make that illumination possible. First, I feel it imperative to state upfront, that I am most likely not going to say anything that is wholly "new," though the overarching message may be. It may be new to the reader but the thoughts, ideas, and information, be it historical or ecological, will generally speaking have origins elsewhere. I am merely attempting to compile data to support my thesis which is that applying the Golden Rule and by extension, the greatest

3. NASA, "Global Climate Change: Effects"
4. Craffert, *The Life of a Galilean Shaman*, xiii.

commandment[5], as a matter of course will make the planet more habitable, sustainable, just, happy, and pleasant for all concerned. With that caveat in mind, I will make my case for "Going Golden."

I am doubtless not the only person to ever come to the conclusion that the Golden Rule's broad application would be of great benefit to humanity. That said, my road to getting to that point is unique because, as is true for everyone, I experience the world from a perspective that is uniquely my own. A wise woman once told me, in response to my angst over experiencing a spiritual practice in a far different way than anything I had read about, that, "1000 people could walk down Prince Street at exactly the same time and each one will have a different experience." My unique perspective is shaped by my social location, a term used by theologians, pastors, biblical scholars, sociologists, and others as a means of identifying the lens through which we see the world, engage people, and do academic work. Briefly then, my social location is a white American male, in my mid-40s, in the working-class tax bracket, with both a bachelor's degree in history from a state university, and a M.A. in religion from a progressive United Church of Christ Seminary. Additionally, I am heterosexual, have been married more than once, and am a member of a theologically and socially progressive mainline Protestant church. I am paying a mortgage on our first home, and am a disabled veteran, living in the mid-Atlantic region of the United States. All of these things shape the perspective through which I see the world.

From childhood through early adulthood and into my 30s, I was a practicing Christian of the fundamentalist Southern Baptist variety whose theological views were mixed with conservative Church of Christ doctrine taught me by well meaning, though theologically unschooled, grandparents. That said, I was not a very good Christian, at least according to my own guilty feelings for sins of omission or commission, whether they were real or imagined, and based on the harsh judgments of others who were quick to point out my failings in sin management. These doctrinal teachings and the resultant guilt, fed by a hell-based fear that created a traumatizing theological view, and thoughts of sinfulness still shape me in terms of being "embedded theologies" that can creep into my thought processes and generate further questions about my spiritual and world view.[6] In the early part of this century, I began to have serious questions about the Southern

5. See Luke 10:25–37.

6. Doehring, *The Practice of Pastoral Care*, 187.

Baptist beliefs I had been living within for so long and was teetering on losing my religion completely. My now ex-wife, whom I will call "Amanda" for purposes of anonymity, at that time was an active duty chaplain in the U.S Army, and I was a non-traditional student using my veteran's benefits to work towards a degree in history while also being a stay-at-home dad. The collegiate studies I was then involved in began to seriously undermine my previously narrow-minded notions of how the world works, who the good guys are, and the idea that there is only one right way to live if one wanted to enter the Kingdom of Heaven after shedding one's mortal coil. Theologically speaking, everything that I had been taught was geared towards the afterlife rather than the here and now, where people are actively suffering. The questioning that arose within my brain as I began to apply the critical thinking skills I had gained during my undergraduate studies from learning to do historical analysis, the academic study of literature, and the occasional classroom debate was seriously confusing to one who had been indoctrinated to think in the impossibly strict binary terms of black and white regarding life as a Christian American fundamentalist.

Amanda was concerned by my new found questioning but assured me that it was only a phase that many Christians go through when going pursuing higher education and that it would pass in time and then my faith would be renewed. The problem arose however, that the more I learned as a student of history, the more I saw that both the fundamentalist Christian doctrines and patriotic rhetoric I had believed for so long were incongruent in many cases with the actual actions engaged in by self-proclaimed Christians and the U.S. as a national entity. The teachings of Jesus were either ignored or glossed over completely as spiritual notions for the afterlife in many instances in favor of a doctrine that reflects the conflation of Christianity with Empire that began in the fourth century when Constantine put crosses on his banners and went to war.[7] My personal Christian theology then began to shift from sin management and the afterlife to become more rooted in what I saw as the essence of Christ's ethical teachings, his greatest commandment, to love the Creator and to love others as one loves oneself, along with his articulation of the Golden Rule to "do unto others as you would have them do unto you."[8]

---

7. Zahnd, *A Farewell to Mars*, 28,33.

8. Jesus taught that these were in fact the most important aspects of living a Godly life. See the parable of the Good Samaritan in Luke 10:25–37.

The slope got slipperier until I reached a personal breaking point one day in the lead up to the second invasion of Iraq in 2003. I had been attending a Protestant chapel services on the army base regularly despite the confusion swirling in my mind. During the times devoted to prayer requests, chapel members (soldiers and their spouses) would voice their concerns and needs that they wanted prayer for. Multiple times people had asked for a swift victory for America in the event of yet another war with a country far from our shores that was (and is) completely incapable of invading the United States or bombing it into oblivion with intercontinental ballistic missiles. It was Empire Christianity pure and simple wedded with runaway American nationalism. Not once did anyone stand up to invoke the Gospel of Matthew chapter 5 verse 9 (Blessed are the peacemakers) and pray that no war would be fought and that the poor people of the Middle East could experience peace. Nor did anyone ever ask to pray for the Iraqi citizens whose lives would be turned upside down by the invasion to topple a ruthless dictator, who for years had been propped up by the American government and who had for so long served "American interests"[9] in the region so well. Despite ruminating on this during a service one morning, in my confusion and fear, I remained silent, afraid at that time to rock the boat or perhaps make Amanda, who was the chaplain presiding over the service, look bad. I failed to use my prophetic voice out of fear.[10]

A week later, I was putting out materials for a Sunday School class for elementary school aged kids. As I placed the materials on the table before the class, Amanda was talking to me in the classroom about the forthcoming lesson. What followed is something that I will likely remember for the rest of my life. A staff sergeant came into the room and in extremely animated voice proclaimed, "Bush has had enough. We're going to war, baby!" Immediately and wordlessly, I placed the remaining Sunday School literature for six and seven seven-year-old kids on the table, turned on my heels and walked out of the chapel without ever looking back or offering an explanation. I refused to go to church after this event for well over a decade. From then on, I began to explore other faith traditions and

9. This term is often coded language for economic interests that amount to taking resources or getting unfair economic advantages that benefit American companies while leaving the local population high and dry. For more see: Perkins' *Confessions of an Economic Hitman,* or study the overthrow of Guatemalan President Jacobo Arbenz by the CIA so that United Fruit Company could protect its profit margins by not paying taxes on the land they were using to grow and export bananas.

10. For more on prophetic voice, McMickle, *Where Have All the Prophets Gone.*

began the process of healing from the traumatic experience of believing the hellfire and brimstone, Judgment Day condemnation, guilt mongering version of fundamentalist Christianity I had been force fed from childhood into adulthood. For years, I had no idea that there were other ways to be a Christian.

A few years after my walk-out (which Amanda took personally and, in some measure, inched our truly awful marriage closer towards a divorce in 2004), my life took another important turn as I accompanied a friend in September of 2007 to "The Farm," an intentional community with a working ecovillage, in Summertown, TN to learn about something revolutionary called permaculture design. This course turned out to be a life changing event that has since informed my thinking, my behavior, and my life in big and small ways.

An Australian academic named Bill Mollison and one of his students, David Holmgren, co-originated the design science that they called permaculture in the 1970s in response to growing ecological problems and the need for sustainable, regenerative ways to manage land and water in cooperation with the natural world. Creating cultivated ecosystems that provide for the needs of humanity while simultaneously serving all life, from soil microbes to the tallest trees, is one of the primary goals of creating a good permaculture design.[11] Informing their system of design are principles and ethics. The ethics as stated by Holmgren in his excellent book, *Permaculture: Principles and Pathways Beyond Sustainability*, are Earth Care, People Care, and Redistribute the Surplus/set limits to consumption. Many permaculture enthusiasts state the ethics slightly differently to Holmgren. My own version of the permaculture ethics is stated in a more theological way: Creation Care, Neighbor Care, and Future Care.

In addition to these ethics, there are a number of principles permaculture designers and practitioners attempt to follow when they design a system, be it a kitchen garden, a food forest, or an entire community. One of these principles, about which more will be said in Chapter Seven, is to design from patterns to details. To design a system in this way means to make a detailed an assessment of the major patterns that are prevalent at the site being designed. For instance, before digging up the soil and putting in a garden or crop, a permaculture designer would want to know about the topography, where the water flows on-site, what type of soil is present,

---

11. Mollison, *Permaculture: A Designer's Manual*, ix.

the climatic characteristics of the bioregion[12] where the site is located, the solar aspect, the direction of the prevailing winds and the once in a century storms or other powerful events that occur at less frequent intervals that can disrupt a design site and adversely affect yields. These are the patterns; the garden is one of the site details. Observing and learning the patterns can save a lot of sweat later for those working that land. As permies[13] like to say, "Observation saves perspiration."

Permaculture, goes far beyond landscape and agricultural systems design. It can be used to design a community, school, business, or almost any aspect of a society. Our culture has patterns that keep repeating and many of these patterns are all too often negative. Poverty, corruption, crime, war, along with selfishness and greed are rampant because we have failed to heed important patterns. One of these vitally important patterns is the existence of a maxim akin to The Golden Rule[14] which is found in all of humanity's major religious faiths and wisdom traditions.[15] Sages and spiritual teachers from vastly different cultures have come to the conclusion that "doing unto others as you would have them do unto you" would create a better culture and society. To me, that points to the Golden Rule's significance for all of humanity and informs how I want to live my life. What follows will be an examination of various aspects of our culture and potential alternatives based upon following the Golden Rule and Jesus' greatest commandment, which he said is to love our neighbors as ourselves, as I understand them.

12. A bioregion is a geographical region that can be defined by watersheds, topography, geographic features, and cultural characteristics. For more info see. Thayer, *Life-Place: Bioregional Thought and Practice*.

13. A nickname for permaculturist.

14. For Christians, the Golden Rule is found in Matthew 7:12.

15. Even Satanists have a rule of reciprocity. See: http://www.religioustolerance.org/reciproc2.htm

2.

Down on the Farm
An Examination of Industrial Agriculture

MODERN INDUSTRIAL AGRICULTURAL PRACTICES are based upon myopic definitions of efficiency (i.e. higher profit margins without regard to anything else) and the flawed logic of seeking increased yields from inert dirt that has been drenched in a variety of chemicals or by perpetually trying to decrease the physical space needed for these so-called farms. Advertisers who market products made from the cereal grains grown on conventional monocropped farms, such as breads, pasta, and so on, along with meat, eggs, and dairy products would have us believe that their products' points of origin are idyllic farms with verdant green rolling hills with happy animals grazing in the sun, or that the amber waves of grain are similarly bucolic instead of being toxically produced to withstand being sprayed with RoundUp. The marketing belies the truth of industrialized farming. As permaculture designer and educator Geoff Lawton notes, modern farming is more like mining than agriculture because it turns living soil ecosystems into inert, hard pan dirt, and creates pollution from chemical runoff and the highly concentrated manures from livestock production.[1]

Animals produced for meat or dairy products are most often raised in combined animal feeding operations (CAFOs) in which hundreds, if not thousands, of animals are kept in as small as space possible.[2] CAFOs generate vast amounts of pollution due to the high concentrations of manure generated from packing as many animals into as small a space as pos-

1. Lawton, "Permaculture: Greening the Desert."
2. Sierra Club, "Why are CAFOs Bad?"

sible on those sites, which then pollutes watersheds due to run-off during rainfall events.[3] This overcrowding creates appalling conditions that in turn generate numerous unnecessary health problems for the animals and results in many deaths. Chickens have their beaks removed to prevent them from pecking each other to death due to the stress of overcrowding[4] either in battery cages or in long enclosed barns and from being forced to hyperproduce eggs or meat. The broiler birds used for meat have now been bred to have such outlandishly sized breasts that often they lose the ability to walk as they are too top heavy. These birds often remain seated in their own filth and then lose feathers and develop sores from being stationary. Commercially reared turkeys cannot even breed naturally due to being too big breasted.[5] With poultry, their breeding and confinement farming ensure that the bird's lives are a nightmarish existence. If we are what we eat, then to eat factory farm raised poultry products is to eat abject animal suffering.

Pigs fare no better than the poultry. Sows give birth to litters of piglets in cramped farrowing pens (a pen where sows give birth away from other pigs) so small that the mothers cannot get up and move around. Those piglets end up inside long metal barns that are mechanized versions of a fecal and urine drenched hell. After being fattened up and injected with antibiotics, they are most often shipped to a slaughterhouse to be unceremoniously killed at a dangerously high pace. Colorado State University Professor of Animal Science, Dr. Temple Grandin, has shown that the slaughterhouse environment is tremendously stressful because the animals, already afraid because they are in a new environment, are forced to move with electric prods that shock the animals before they are processed in a cacophony of noise and an atmosphere of fear.[6] This is all done as fast as possible by overworked, underpaid employees whose jobs are very dangerous due to the knives being wielded, the breakneck pace that "must" be kept up, and the resultant fatigue of long hours spent in hyperactivity.[7]

Cattle in America are often put into feedlots to be "finished" (fattened for slaughter) in enormous numbers[8] to stand on packed dirt and manure

3. Hribar, "Understanding Concentrated Animal Feeding Operations and their Impact on Communities."

4. Poultry Hub," Beak Trimming."

5. Kingsolver, Hopp, and Kingsolver, *Animal, Vegetable, Miracle.*

6. Grandin, "Stress and Meat Quality."

7. See: Schlosser, *Fast Food Nation.*

8. Cattle Empire, "In the Heart of the Beef Feeding."

which often leads to painful issues with their hooves, including a serious condition known as hoof rot. Dairy cattle too are kept this way on large commercial dairies rather than grazing picturesquely on verdant pastures of lush grass and legumes.[9] They are fed a diet of genetically modified (GMO) corn and soybean-based feeds along with other byproducts of industrial agriculture that they did not evolve to eat, but that will fatten them up more quickly or stimulate dairy cows to produce inordinate amounts of milk. It's similar to people eating too much junk food. For cattle, corn and soybeans are junk food. Grasses and leguminous hay, such as alfalfa, are what cattle thrive on and when managed appropriately. cattle (and other grazing animals) can be a tremendous asset to the soil and grass – based ecosystems helping to regenerate soil and sequester carbon.[10]

Proponents of these CAFO systems proclaim that the feedlots, pig barns, and battery cages are efficient because they lower the monetary costs to produce eggs, milk, and meat in small spaces with as many animals as possible into their facilities, which means more meat for people to eat that is produced as cheaply as possible.[11] Instead of seeing these techniques holistically, they look only to the bottom line of profit. From a broader, more holistic perspective however, they are terribly inefficient in terms of the needed energy inputs (electricity, fossil fuels etc.) and the polluting outputs (toxic agricultural chemicals, antibiotics, and manure) created by such a system. They are a detriment to communities, farmers and ranchers, employees, and the people who eat their meat products. Additionally, CAFOs are environmentally damaging in a way that is impossible to overstate due to the aforementioned concentrations of manure which lead to nitrogen overloads that run off into the water thus contributing to dead zones where rivers drain into salt water such as the Chesapeake Bay or the Gulf

9. In the mid-90s I was herd manager on a commercial dairy in Godley, TX that fed a total mixed ration to cattle kept in feedlot style yards of packed dirt and manure. On one side of the farm the cattle stood on concrete to eat their feed and on the other side on packed earth. The concrete had to be cleaned daily with a front-end loader to remove the manure. Foot rot was a huge problem on the farm. At that time, I treated the foot rot infected cattle with a spray on application of antibiotics that is normally used in poultry waterers for young birds.

10. Savory, "Savory Institute."

11. Hribar, "Understanding Confined Animal Feeding Operations," 2.

of Mexico,[12] not to mention the stench created by the massive amounts of feces piling up which I can personally attest is absolutely vile.

The meat produced in this manner comes from animals in a near constant state of stress due to overcrowding and then later in the slaughterhouse. Dr. Grandin, a proponent of humane slaughter techniques, writes on her website that the level of stress an animal feels prior to slaughter affects the quality of the meat. For example, she notes that in cattle, stressful handling results in a depletion of glycogen, a muscle energy source, from the animal's muscle resulting in something called "dark cutters"[13] which is the term for dark, firm, dry meat in cattle. CAFO raised animals are given large doses of antibiotics to offset illness caused by overcrowded, stressful, and generally unhealthy living conditions. According to the Centers for Disease Control (CDC) overuse of antibiotic medications in agriculture (and elsewhere) leads to the phenomena of "superbugs" that are resistant to antibiotics, which makes treating diseases more difficult[14] and can lead to milk and meat becoming tainted with antibiotics.

In addition to excess antibiotics, dairy cattle are given hormones to increase their milk yield and while I was the herd manager on the large commercial dairy farm in Godley, TX, a place sadly now covered in fracking sites, I personally shot up cows with them. The lactating cattle there lived their lives in pens of hard packed dirt which they left only to be milked twice a day in a barn with a holding pen and milk stanchion with concrete floors. Only when they were dried off (no longer being milked prior to giving birth again) would they be put in the pasture to graze and eat hay as nature intended. One day a young woman fresh from Texas Tech University with a degree in agribusiness came to the dairy to sell us on the idea of giving a growth hormone called bovine somatotropin (BST) to the cattle to improve the milk yield of the herd.[15] She told us that one inexpensive, subcutaneous shot per cow, per month would have those girls pumping out the milk like crazy and be a boon to the farm's owners. Prior to starting this experiment, the herd average was around 33 pounds of milk per day, per cow (milk is sold to processors by the 100 weight rather than in gallons).

12. U.S. Department of Commerce, National Oceanic and Atmospheric Administration, "What is a Dead Zone?"

13. Grandin, "Dark Cutters (DFD)."

14. Philpott, "Many Meat Producers Claim their Operations." see also: Frieden, "Antibiotic Resistance Threats in the United States, 2013."

15. U.S. Food and Drug Administration, "Bovine Somatotropin (BST)."

When I left the farm for employment elsewhere about six months later, the average had doubled to 66 lbs./cow. The yield started climbing as soon as we started giving the cattle those shots.

On the face of it this would seem a great thing for struggling farmers. Digging deeper however, I learned that it is really an awful way to treat the animals because cows are not meant to produce so much milk and doing so is hard on them. The cattle given the BST had absurdly large udders that were painfully distended with all of that extra milk. Some cows gave well in excess of 100 lbs. of milk per day. Using growth hormones also has potential implications for people unwittingly drinking milk laced with the extra hormones, which is why some companies, notably Ben and Jerry's Ice Cream, do not buy milk from farms that use them.[16]

Like animal agriculture, commodity crops such as corn, wheat, and potatoes are also grown and produced in a way that is ecologically unsound, to say the least. Soil, that most important commodity for any nation, is treated profanely as it gets increasingly doused with the various chemicals used in modern farming. As with the high concentrations of manure in animal production, chemically based farming adds excessive nitrogen as well as phosphates to soil to compensate for lost fertility due to poor soil management. Crops are drenched with herbicides like RoundUp, the best-selling herbicide on the planet, that, according to soil ecologist Dr. Elaine Ingham, destroy soil biota (the microscopic life that make healthy soil.)[17] The plants, whether grain producing or vegetable producing, can only take up so much of the nitrogen or phosphorus from the fertilizers which are added to the soil. Much of the rest runs off into the watershed[18] or ends up in the ground water. That runoff inevitably flows downstream and, even more so than the manure generated by CAFOs' animal production, creates eutrophication, a term used when the demand for oxygen increases due to algal blooms caused by all the runoff and causes other aquatic life such as fish end up dying from the lack of oxygen.

Many of the chemicals used in farming applications (or in lawn and garden products) are toxic to humans as well as the environment. Biological engineering of commodity crops has created a new type of crop known as a genetically modified organism (GMO). Biotech companies would have us believe that creating and growing these crops is not only safe but also

16. Ben & Jerry's, "rBGH."
17. Ingham, "Building Soil Health."" See also: Brown, "The Roots of Your Health."
18. For more on watersheds see: Perlman, "What is a Watershed?"

imperative if we are going to feed a growing population. Unfortunately for them, neither of those statements are true. Many GMOs are only altered to be able to withstand the chemical glyphosate, a key component in the most widely used herbicide on Earth. *The International Service for the Acquisition of Agri-Biotech Applications* website has lists for all of the approved GMO crops that can be grown. By far the longest list, with 331 specific crops, is the one listing all of the herbicide tolerant crops such as those that are RoundUp Ready.[19] Glyphosate, which is found in the Monsanto product RoundUp, as well as herbicides from competing companies, is known to be toxic to humans and is now being found in human breast milk,[20] and urine,[21] in rain water, ground water, and surface water[22] because it doesn't simply become inert once sprayed. French scientists from the University of Caen concluded that RoundUp type broadleaf herbicides are dangerous due to the so-called inert ingredients in the formula being toxic to human cells.[23] Researchers from a Norwegian university found extreme levels of RoundUp contamination in soybeans that were grown in Iowa. The abstract for their research also notes that organic soybeans had a better nutritional profile than those grown with chemical inputs.[24]

When a RoundUp Ready crop is sprayed with RoundUp, it doesn't die but does become tainted, as shown by the aforementioned Norwegian study on soybeans, with the chemical that the World Health Organization proclaimed in 2015 to be a "probable carcinogen."[25] Unbeknownst to people shopping at grocery stores around America, these GMO crops laced with RoundUp have been ending up in the produce aisle and in prepackaged foods for years now, so that the buyers who eat them have essentially become unwitting lab rats in a corporately run science experiment without their prior knowledge or permission. Some European nations are starting to ban GMO crops due to the health risk associated with eating food laced with glyphosate. In response to food security issues for people around

19. ISAAA.org, "Advanced Search – : 331 Events Found."

20. The Ecologist, "Glyphosate Found in Breast Milk."

21. Hoppe, "Determination of Glyphosate Residues," 6.

22. Gillam, "U.S. Researchers Find Roundup. " see also: Battaglin, "Glyphosate Herbicide Found in Many Midwestern Streams."

23. Gammon, "Weed-Whacking Herbicide."

24. Bohn, Cuhra, and Traavik, et al, "Compositional Differences in Soybeans on the Market." See also: Gerrard, "High Levels of RoundUp in Soybeans."

25. Loew, "Roundup a 'Probable Carcinogen.'"

the world, the United Nations recently stated in a report produced by the *United Nations Commission on Trade and Development* entitled "Trade and Environment Review 2013: Wake Up Before It's Too Late," that only small scale, organic agriculture can sustainably feed the world, which directly refutes the global agribusiness claim that only more chemical agriculture can do so.[26]

Chemical agriculture is completely unsustainable due to its reliance on enormous inputs of energy in the form of fossil fuels (most synthetic fertilizers are fossil fuel based, in addition to the gasoline and diesel fuel used in running the ever-larger equipment). In this modern, increasingly globalized world, every person currently alive is our neighbor whether they are down the street from our homes or in a village in Bangladesh. Industrialized farming makes it harder for many people to earn a living on the land (see Mexico post NAFTA as an example)[27] because of land use changes and chemicals that are too expensive. In India, some farmers have become so desperate because they had been following the practices of conventional chemically based and genetically modified agriculture, which is lauded by the chemical companies whose profits from selling their toxic concoctions are enormous, that many have ended their lives by drinking the chemicals that were intended for their degraded, unproductive land.[28]

Why would farmers commit suicide in such staggering and heartbreaking numbers? Because, like a heroin junky whose need for the drug increases the longer they have used it, once the soil is depleted it becomes nothing more than inert dirt, meaning more and more expensive chemicals are needed to maintain yields. This creates a cycle of indebtedness where farmers become more ensnared by companies whose only goal is to sell more chemicals. It's a cycle eerily similar to the "company store" model that trapped working class people in debt. With appropriate farming practices, none of these chemicals are needed, according to Dr. Ingham, whose work has shown that crops grown in healthy soil, which teems with life, are more resilient to changing weather conditions such as drought, too much rain, or fluctuating temperatures.

By now, you may be asking yourself, "What does any of this have to do with following the Golden Rule or with loving the Creator, the Creation and

26. UNCTAD, "Wake up Before It Is Too Late."

27. Carlsen, "Under NAFTA, Mexico Suffered."

28. Malone, "The GM Genocide." See also: Pokharel, "Why India's Cotton Farmers are Killing Themselves."

all our neighbors?" I will attempt to connect the various dots of the current agricultural practices so prevalent in the U.S and elsewhere to the theological questions above. Let us begin with the ones producing the commodity crops and other foods (truck farming) as well as the fiber producing plants like cotton and flax that are needed for manufacturing clothing and other goods. Farmers possessed with the knowledge that their farming practices are putting God's creation at risk, as well as risking the health of the people who eat what they have produced, would certainly be in direct violation of the law of reciprocity. *When we know better we can and must do better.* I don't know of anyone who actually *wants* to be poisoned nor do I know of anyone who lives downstream of somewhere (which means most of us) who *wants* to have excessive nutrients and chemical runoff killing the rivers, streams, lakes, and ponds, making the water unfit for drinking or even swimming in, as has happened to the mighty, and ancient Susquehanna River, which flows near to where I currently live.[29] This incredible river is poisoned by all manner of pollution, including agricultural pollution, meaning that a tremendous source of natural capital (renewable and non-renewable resources that are provided by ecosystems and facilitate human survival, such as a fishery)[30] is now producing fish with cankers on their bodies among other water quality problems.

Anyone who eats food and wants to follow the Golden Rule, and who is now possessed with this knowledge, should eat organically and locally if it is economically feasible to do so, with the knowledge that so doing supports farmers who are doing their best to create healthy soil (literally an indispensable natural resource) and healthful food without polluting their bioregion or "life place" (the geographic, cultural, and or watershed boundary of any given area).[31] By extension, those organic producers are *not* buying toxic chemicals from the agribusiness conglomerates whose products are now destroying the ecological systems that perpetuate life, thus making it more difficult for humanity to sustain life, especially the poor whom Jesus called "the least of these" saying that whatever we do to them, we do to him. Similarly, buying meat from local sources who raise free range chickens or grass-fed cattle, hogs, or sheep makes CAFOs less viable, again helping those who live downstream and those who live near the

29. Reilly, "How Sick is the Susquehanna?"

30. BusinessDictionary.com, "What is Natural Capital? "

31. Thayer, *LifePlace: Bioregional Thought and Practice*, 3.

overpowering smells of a factory chicken producer, hog farm, commercial dairy, or a feedlot.[32]

There are alternatives to chemical based, GMO agriculture and the CAFO model. These techniques and practices can actually regenerate soil, and clean the water and the air. The work of the Rodale Institute in Kutztown, PA has shown the efficacy of regenerating the soil and growing food organically in a multi-decade long, side by side study, comparing conventional chemical agriculture with organic methods. Their research has shown that the soil recovers from the abuses of conventional, chemical intensive methods when replaced with regenerative farming practices.[33] Properly done, organic practices can bring the soil back to a healthy state and keep it in place, rather than losing uncovered topsoil to wind and water driven erosion. The Rodale team has found that the organic plots begin to outperform chemically maintained land after about the fifth year of soil regeneration, especially in times of drought or too much rain. This latter point is especially important in light of the current change in climatic patterns and the resultant prolonged droughts and torrential rain fall events that are on the rise. Resiliency in agriculturally productive systems in the face of climate change is imperative if enough food is to be grown to support a growing population.

Grazing animals should be raised on pasture rather than in feedlots. Well known farmers such as Joel Salatin (author of *You Can Farm: The Entrepreneur's Guide to Start & Succeed in a Farming Enterprise* and several other books) in Virginia and Mark Shepard (author of *Restoration Agriculture*) in Wisconsin are achieving fantastic results through appropriate land stewardship methods such as rotational grazing, alley cropping (planting fruit, nut, and timber trees between grazing paddocks), diversity of products called "value adding," and paying close attention to animal and human welfare. As Sheppard notes in the film *INHABIT: A Permaculture Perspective*[34] his animals only have one bad day, which just so happens to be their last day. Using rotational grazing or intensive grazing management can fast forward the regeneration of healthy soil and a help create a cleaner watershed. Incorporating trees reduces the amount of carbon dioxide in the air as well as adding fruit and nut crops or valuable timber for future use.

---

32. For excellent fiction related to agricultural topics covered in this chapter see: Ozeki, *My Year of Meats*; Ozeki, *All Over Creation*; Proulx, *That Old Ace in the Hole*.

33. Rodale Institute, "The Farming Systems Trial," 3–13.

34. Boutsikirkis, *INHABIT: A Permaculture Perspective*.

Removing carbon dioxide from the Earth's atmosphere is of paramount importance as we are now above 400 parts per million (ppm) of it in the atmosphere and we need to be at 350 ppm or below to maintain a stable climate.[35] Trees on farms are beneficial for a variety of reasons such as improving the soil through leaf drop and root die off, aeration of the soil from the root penetration, and through symbiotic relationships with fungi in which the trees and fungi communicate in order to move nutrients to where they are needed through the fungal mycelium.[36] Our farms need more trees, especially along rivers, streams, and other waterways.

Permaculture and regenerative farming techniques applied to broad-acre agriculture have profound impacts on soil formation, water retention, drought proofing, and increased biodiversity. Practitioners such as Geoff Lawton, Darren Doherty, Sepp Holzer, and my friend Cliff Davis in Tennessee, amongst others use strategies such as keyline plowing[37] (an off contour ripping of the soil which creates a landscape where every drop of rain that falls is kept on the farm rather than running off), digging swales on contour (essentially a ditch that is dead level, which allows water to collect in it and slowly percolate into the soil that then creates an envelope of water that slowly flows through the soil downhill) and systems of ponds and dams to hold water in the soil which increases fertility, drought resistance, and soil biodiversity. Different strategies are effective in different landscapes and the results are often stunning as is evidenced by Lawton's work in the profoundly hot and dry Middle Eastern nation of Jordan.[38] We need to implement these types of strategies throughout the American grain belt to recharge the Ogallala Aquifer, which has been dangerously depleted from over irrigation. This aquifer stretches from the panhandle of Texas to southern South Dakota and is the single most important aquifer in the United States. If it dries up, the entire "breadbasket of America" will no

35. 350.org "A Global Campaign to Confront the Climate Crisis."

36. I am indebted to Dave Jacke for his work on edible forest gardens as well as other permaculture teachers who have shared their knowledge of forest-based ecosystems with me. See: Jacke and Toensmeier, *Edible Forest Gardens*, vol. 1; Jacke and Toensmeier, *Edible Forest Gardens*, vol. II.; Also see: Stamets, *Mycelium Running*.

37. A technique pioneered in Australia in the 20th century by P.A. Yeomans. See: Yeomans and Yeomans, *Water for Every Farm: Yeomans Keyline Plan*.

38. Lawton, " Permaculture: Greening the Desert."

longer support growing the grain that grows throughout the Great Plains states.[39]

As previously mentioned, the United Nations has reported that only small scale, organic agriculture can feed the world. The industrial model has called for bigger and bigger farms with more and more consolidation of land into fewer and fewer hands. In this age of rapidly declining fossil fuel resources,[40] following the industrial model is a recipe for disaster. We need to localize agriculture in order to drastically shorten the supply chain (it's absurd for example that California provides so much of America's produce) and to provide meaningful livelihoods for people. Local economies thrive when more people are working for local farms and the enterprises such as cooperative distribution centers, greengrocers, and supermarkets that are supplied by them. Community is fostered, as well, when we get to know who is growing our food, which is impossible if the salad greens and hamburgers are produced hundreds, if not thousands, of miles away. Getting to know our local neighbors is a great way to love them as well as create resilient community groups.

We must also hold our political representatives accountable for creating this mess to begin with. They are beholden to what theologian Walter Wink dubbed the Domination System of principalities and powers that undergird nations, economic systems, political parties, institutions, and other elements of civilization.[41] Too often, they *kowtow* to big business, thus paving the way for all sorts of abuses while distracting voters with wedge issues that supposedly show how "Godly" or "patriotic" they are, when all the while cancer rates are skyrocketing and the biosphere is on the verge of collapse. The Farm Bill is often a handout to large corporate agribusiness to subsidize the growth of genetically modified commodity crops like corn and soybeans, while organic producers are often hindered by absurd regulations,[42] expensive fees for certification, and the seeming high price of

---

39. Frantz, "Ogallala Aquifer Initiative." See also: Amelinckx, "Where Has All the Water Gone?"

40. Deffeyes, "Hubbert's Peak, The Peak." All fossil fuel sources are dwindling which explains the mad rush to get as much as possible from the ground regardless of ecological and societal costs. Environmentally dangerous practices such as fracking and tar sands extraction remain legal in spite of known pollution and even earthquakes associated with these techniques.

41. Wink, *Engaging the Powers*, 6,9.

42. Joel Salatin writes extensively on this subject. See his book entitled, *Everything I Want to Do is Illegal.*

their products (often due to subsidies received by chemically maintained farms but denied to producers of real food).

Part of the purpose of this chapter is to name the powers, as Wink insists must be done, so that people can then engage the powers of the capitalist system in a nonviolent way,[43] thereby making life more livable and the planet more habitable for all people, especially the most vulnerable, wherever they may reside. The Golden Rule as I read it is all about human rights. As is showing love to our neighbors. Clean air, healthy soil, clean water, and healthful foods are human rights. A habitable biosphere is a human right. We cannot have those for everyone while chemically intensive crop production and CAFO livestock production are the norm, and that won't change as long as politicians willfully mislead the public about GMOs and ignore the effects of peak oil, peak soil, and the chemical contamination that is a huge byproduct of chemical agribusiness and conventional farming.

43. Wink, *Engaging the Powers*, 289.

3.

Let's Go Shopping
Consumer Culture in America

SHOPPING IS PRACTICALLY A national sport in America. Almost every week there is a "Huge Sale" to tempt people to come to the closest big box retailer or mall to spend their hard-earned money. No holiday, regardless of what is ostensibly being celebrated, seems to happen without yet another three-day sale. Some of these are disgusting, such as Columbus Day Sales, where we are enticed to save money while celebrating the actions of a man who committed horrific atrocities and genocide against the docile native Arawak inhabitants of the island he stumbled upon.[1] Or the profanely manic Christmas sales on the aptly named "Black Friday," where people can now routinely be seen trampling over people or fighting with others in order to save a few bucks, while supposedly preparing to celebrate the birth of one who taught that people should be non-violent and to give their wealth to the poor.[2] Such is the import of shopping for things that we most often have no actual real or pressing need for to the economy that former President (and current at large war criminal)[3] George W. Bush said in the aftermath of the alleged terrorist attacks on the World Trade Center and Pentagon that to get back to normalcy Americans should "go shopping."[4] In 2001, I remember doing just that at a mall in El Paso, Texas in the days following the collapse of the buildings.

1. Zinn and Arnove, *A People's History of the United States*, 1–5.
2. Matthew 19:16–22 is one such example.
3. Ridley, "Bush Convicted of War Crimes in Absentia."
4. Fox, "A Look Back at Bush's Economic Missteps."

Consumers buying things is a key indicator to the health of the economy,[5] that near mythic, yet intangible thing with its "invisible hand of the market" that politicians, business people, and bankers worship like the Golden Calf of the Israelites. Yet, to buy things, whether needed or not, is to consume resources, and these resources that especially those of us in developed nations are consuming at such alarming rates, are finite. The voracious cycle of consumption, buy it, use it, and then dispose of it, is having a profoundly detrimental effect on the planet and its inhabitants, especially those who are poor. As will be shown, this is not news to policy makers, yet they intentionally perpetuate this system of conspicuous, unequal consumption and the poverty that it engenders to maintain the status quo of the American standard of living here in the U.S. and in other countries that aspire to our level of conspicuous consumption.

Consider that during World War II, while rationing was in place, people were encouraged to grow victory gardens, and anything that could be recycled, repaired, or reused, was in fact recycled, repaired, or reused in the name of national defense. Not so in these days of perpetual warfare and conspicuous consumption. Furthermore, to ensure the highest possible profit margins, manufacturers, distributors, and retailers are constantly seeking ways to cut costs, often at the expense of human rights and dignity, living wages, and devastating environmental degradation in order to lure more customers to buy ever more cheaply produced consumer goods and to burn more oil.[6] What's wrong with this picture? How would the world change if people applied the Golden Rule and made every effort to "Love our neighbors as we love ourselves" when deciding to make purchases and from whom? These are the questions that will be explored throughout this chapter.

From a global perspective, the current economic system is outrageously flawed because billions of people are left out, as is evidenced by the continued concentration of wealth into certain countries while resources are acquired through force, and politicians work to keep it that way. Capitalism is predicated upon creating profits, the bigger the better, seemingly at any cost, without regard to human needs, resource scarcity, or ecological impact. Another way to say that is that capitalism is by definition "the love

5. Perry, "4 Key Indicators That Move Markets."

6. Volf, *Flourishing*, 16, 39–42. For more information, one can search for stories on the internet regarding modern slavery such as in Thailand's seafood industry and cacao growing in Africa, sweatshops in a variety of industries and environmental damage done by extractive industries due to issues such as fracking wastes.

of money" which the Christian Bible teaches is "the root of all evil."[7] This love of money is responsible for creating an enormous disparity between the rich and poor, so much so that billions of people globally are living in abject poverty in developing nations.[8] Take a second to let the following information sink in, eighty percent of the people on Earth live on less than ten dollars a day,[9] while most of the people fortunate enough to live in wealthy nations have it comparatively easy in terms of having enough food, clean water, and shelter. For many people in America, ten dollars is not enough to cover the expense of daily coffees, eating out, or buying snacks. By global standards, an annual income of $34,000 puts one in the top one percent, while in America that makes one middle class.[10]

While growing up in rural north Texas I experienced what many in America would consider poverty, yet I never missed a meal, never had to go without clean water, and never had to sleep on the street until I made the choice to leave home. In the house that I lived in throughout junior high and most of high school, cats could literally enter my sister's room from the crawlspace under the house by crawling through a hole in the floor, and the roof leaked copiously in multiple places; yet we had a roof over our heads and food on the table. We were considered poor because we often wore hand-me-down clothing, never had a new car, and my mom sold eggs and took in ironing to make ends meet. How different would my life have been had I been born poor in someplace like Guatemala, Botswana, Afghanistan, or Bolivia?

The system is skewed in favor of the "Haves" and against the "Have Nots" and is geared to maintaining that disparity of wealth and power. It is an economy run by the Domination System as theologian Walter Wink terms it.[11] Capitalism is fed by the spiritual essence of greed, and "might makes right."[12] This creates abuses of power, that lead to environmental degradation, human rights abuses such as slavery and human trafficking[13],

7. 1 Timothy 6:7--10 says we should be content with food, clothing, and shelter because the love of money is the root of all kinds of evil.

8. 25% of the world's population lives on less than $1/day and 2.8 billion live on less than $2/day. See: Houry, "World Poverty Quiz."

9. Shah, "Poverty Facts and Stats."

10. Kenny, "We're All the 1 Percent."

11. Wink, *Engaging the Powers*, 9.

12. Wink, *Engaging the Powers*, 16.

13. Hard numbers are difficult to pin down but there are tens of millions of people trapped in slavery as of 2017. Greenberg, "Are 27 Million People Trapped in Modern

the furthering of poverty, and costly imperialism[14] that allows nations like the U.S. to take control of resources in other countries and thereby create and control wealth.[15] This is often done by force of arms (to Wink's "might makes right" point) in order to allow Americans to live in comparative ease and luxury at the expense of people far away as can be seen currently in the Middle East and Latin America to name just two examples. The *Pax Americana* idea, modeled on the Roman Empire's *Pax Romana* model wherein peace and law and order were maintained through violent imperial expansion, creates the illusion of relative peace at home while fostering the military domination of the "provinces," all in the name of "protecting our freedom." It creates an economy that is predicated upon perpetual economic growth despite the limited natural resources available on the planet.[16] That it is impossible to have infinite growth with finite resources is something politicians avoid talking about because that would mean intentionally halting economic growth and asking people to make sacrifices, which Americans as a society are not generally in the habit of doing anymore. Something has got to give, and soon. Our neighbors in foreign countries are every bit as much our neighbors as those who live on the same block as us or in the same town. Many of these people are suffering directly as a result of the mindless consumption of Americans (and other wealthy countries) that perpetuates rampant inequality globally.[17]

Let's move from this "big picture" perspective to more specific ways in which the model currently in use leads us to ignore "doing unto others as we would have them do unto us." When we go shopping we buy all manner of products from clothing and shoes to foodstuffs. We buy tools, electronic gadgets, books and magazines, furniture, building materials, toys, and plastic, tons and tons of petrochemical-based plastic, most of which does not get recycled.[18] Part of my goal is to get readers to think about their shopping habits and the things they buy. Where do these things come from? How are they made (is there mining or other extractive industry involved, does the

---

Slavery?"

14. Sachs, "The Fatal Expense of American Imperialism. "

15. As one example see: Juhasz, "Why the War in Iraq was Fought for Big Oil."

16. For more information see: McKibben, *Deep Economy.*

17. Kochhar, "How Americans Compare with the Global Middle Class."

18. Enormous amounts of plastic waste are contaminating our planet. Microscopic plastic particles are being found in ocean fish and there are huge amounts of plastic garbage floating in the Pacific Ocean as well as other large bodies of water. See: NOAA, "How Big Is the Great Pacific Garbage Patch?"

product contain a lot of chemicals, and so on) and by whom? Do we actually need what we're buying? Are they made to last, or are they disposable?

Clothing is a basic necessity. In many places in the developed world going around nude in public will get people arrested. Clothing protects us from the elements and sometimes helps to identify a person as having a certain type of job— such as those in medical professions, public safety, or public works employees amongst others. For some people, it works for them to have a modest appearance or helps them to maintain a religious identity, such as Hasidic Jews, Sikhs, Rastafarians, the Amish, and some members of the clergy. For others, clothing is used to express their unique personality or helps them to identify with a certain "tribe" such as fans of sports teams, different sub-cultures, or a geographic region such as the American West, where cowboy boots and hats remain commonplace. Sometimes clothing is a part of expressing a person's creativity and personality. Clothes and shoes are rightfully seen as basic necessities and as extensions of who we are. All too often in consumer culture though, our clothes and shoes are just signs of conspicuous consumption, and their points of origin and means of manufacture are hugely problematic if we consider the lived experience of those impoverished and overworked people who are making it all.

Bangladesh, Haiti, Honduras, Viet Nam, Cambodia, China, El Salvador, and Mexico are just some of the countries where a great deal of our clothing is coming from these days. In the current era where we remain under the illusion that fossil fuel energy is cheap,[19] it is seen as sound economic and business policy to ship the items long distances rather than to pay workers a living wage in America or Western Europe for example. I recall television personality Kathy Lee Gifford expressing shock at learning the line of clothing she endorsed for Wal-Mart was made in a Central American sweatshop by thirteen and fourteen-year-olds working twenty hours per day. Having previously denied the allegations, she cried on national television when the evidence that the impoverished kids who were making her richer were working in nearly intolerable conditions was made public.[20] Michael Jordan, the mega-millionaire former basketball star took a different tack. When confronted about the working conditions for the workers making his popular line of Nike Air Jordan shoes, he said that he

19. Fossil fuels are incredibly expensive due to the ecological damage and impacts on human health caused by extracting, refining, and burning them. The International Monetary Fund puts that cost at $5.3 trillion per year. See: Wernick, "IMF: 'True cost' of Fossil Fuels."

20. Strom, "A Sweetheart Becomes Suspect."

was"just trying to do his job," which was to make himself and Phil Knight, the co-founder and former CEO of Nike, incredibly rich, as if the people making the shoes for below poverty level wages were somehow less worthy of fair treatment.[21] How truly ironic for a black man from the American South to hold such a view. In essence, he became what black people have fought against for centuries. He chose to move from being an oppressed person in the American South, to a global oppressor of the poor, enriching himself at the expense of poor factory workers in Nike's factories.[22]

As Secretary of State, Hillary Clinton ran the State Department, which conducted negotiations with Haiti to ensure that the Haitian minimum wage would remain at well under fifty cents an /hour after the Haitian government had passed an increase to sixty-two cents an /hour or five dollars and eleven cents a day. U.S. politicians and diplomats conspired with Haitian elites to keep wages artificially low for already impoverished Haitian workers.[23] Americans got cheaper clothes as a result, and the Haitian people got used as pawns in a game of economic chess. The point is not whether or not Secretary Clinton was directly involved, but rather that this is the sort of collusion I spoke of earlier in this chapter. Collusion of this type is evil, or as Wink would term it, "Satanic" because it intentionally harms others in order to enrich a few.[24] The Haitian garment workers are our neighbors just like someone living right next door to us and we are called to treat them as we would like to be treated. Personally, I hate being used or treated as unworthy of human dignity, and when I work for others I will only work for fair wages. Since that is what I want for myself, and I am sure you do too, then theologically speaking, I must want the same thing for others. It's that simple and we certainly cannot show them love by maintaining a system that keeps them in abject poverty.

By continuing to purchase sweatshop made clothing, we are giving our consent to the manufacturers, distributors, retailers, and their political allies, to continue abusing both people and the environment. The so called "Free Trade Agreements" that rich nations set up are criticized because critics believe that they are enacted to ensure that labor costs are low,[25] and

21. Herbert, "In America; Nike's Pyramid Scheme."
22. For more on not becoming what we hate, see Wink, *Engaging the Powers,* 195–208.
23. teleSUR English. "Haitian Workers Fight."
24. Wink, *Naming the Powers,* 104–105.
25. Marshall, "The Implications of the North American Free Trade." See also: Scott, "Free Trade in the Americas."

that regulations, be they labor or environmentally related, can be either skirted easily or avoided altogether.[26] When the North American Free Trade Agreement (NAFTA) was enacted, many Americans lost their jobs[27], as companies moved across the border into Mexico to make their goods. Maquiladoras (sweatshops) sprang up in border cities such as Ciudad de Juarez and Nuevo Laredo where labor was ridiculously cheap and workers had far fewer rights. Conditions in the maquiladoras were often abysmal for those unfortunate enough to work there especially in the summer heat.[28] I doubt whether most consumers even blinked. Rather, we just kept buying what they were selling, due to our collective naivety or perhaps even callousness that comes from living in such a monolithic seeming economic model that seems impossible to change because it is so pervasive.

There are some inroads being made in terms of ethically made clothing, but one has to be prepared to search for it and to spend comparatively more money to purchase it (though the actual 'real' cost is likely less). When we spend more on clothes, we will most likely buy less clothing, which is a good thing, because so much clothing ends up in landfills due to its highly disposable nature[29] and the fact that some retailers will intentionally damage unsold clothing, toss it into a dumpster, and then claim it all as a loss for tax purposes.[30] Searching for ethically made clothing and shoes can be done by typing into a search engine descriptors such as: 'ethically made clothes,' 'union made clothes/shoes,' 'organic clothing,' 'no sweatshop,' or 'made in America' (simply because we at least have some labor laws here). Look for Fair Trade items in shops or items made from entrepreneurs as well on sites like etsy.com. This ensures that the people making the items are treated with dignity and earn a living wage for their work.[31] The price on the tag

---

26. Cooper, "Free Trade Agreements."

27. Scott, "The High Price of 'Free' Trade."

28. I am indebted to cultural anthropologist, Melissa S. Hunt, whose graduate research on the maquiladora industries in Nueva Laredo, Mexico in 2003 informs this chapter.

29. Zarroli, "In Trendy World of Fast Fashion."

30. Dwyer, "Where Unsold Clothes Meet." See also: Ben-Achour, "What Do Stores Do?"

31. I recently needed to replace my worn out blue jeans and found All American Clothing Company's website. Their jeans are made in the U.S. by union workers using American grown cotton. The prices are comparable to jeans purchased at the mall. http://www.allamericanclothing.com/

may be higher, but if we make the choice to only buy something when it is actually needed we can also save money while applying the Golden Rule.

In late 1997, I moved to England and shortly thereafter found work on a commercial goat dairy farm. The house that we moved into had no closets, only a built-in wardrobe about 6 inches deep and wide enough for two suits to fit side by side. When I mentioned this at work by asking "where are all my clothes supposed to go?" one of the other employees, who wore the same thing every day of the week under his farm coveralls, simply looked at me and said with no trace of irony, "You have too many clothes." I'd never really thought of it that way before and felt like the amount of clothes I had was reasonable, though I had more clothes than I could ever wear in a week. Nowadays I think more in terms of how many items of clothing and how many pairs of shoes do I really need? Would it be the end of the world to wear something more than one day in a row or even one "fashion" season in a row? The answer to both questions is, "No," which is why my current clothing includes some items that are twenty years old and many that I have had for over five years.

These days I have a small chest of drawers devoted to t-shirts, shorts, socks, and underwear. It still seems like a lot to me, though my tendency now is to wear things until they become unserviceable and then cut them up for rags or re-purpose them somehow when possible. If an item is still worth wearing but I get tired of it, I donate it to a thrift store, and then re-place it if need be, often from a thrift store. Recently, I found that the North Face rain jacket I purchased sometime while living in England between 1997 and 1999, was no longer fully water repellant and I would need to replace it after nearly twenty years of rough wear while working on farms, operating heavy equipment, and as my primary outer garment during in-clement weather. In order to live more fully into my values, I decided to try to find a raincoat made with natural materials instead of getting another long lasting, though completely synthetic North Face raincoat. I searched ebay.com for oilskin coats like the ones I had seen while living in England and found an English made Barbour waxed cotton jacket in good condition that someone was selling used. These jackets are well made, long lasting, and can be re-waxed to ensure they stay waterproof. Not only that, it was less expensive than a trip to the local mall for a new synthetic raincoat. It required a shift in my thinking to go from shopping for fun[32] to shopping only when I really need something.

Now I continue to look for ways that I can purchase things that are ethically produced. Sometimes that is well-nigh impossible, which indicates a huge flaw in the system, because of the demon known as greed. Almost two years ago, I began to search for a new pair of running shoes because the shoes I had were wearing out and causing me to stand lopsided. I did an internet search for organic running shoes and came up basically empty. There was a site that listed a few companies, but there were no actual organically produced running shoes available that I could find. My next search was for "eco-friendly" running shoes. Again, some companies came up, but many of the shoes in this category were listed there because they were vegan, which to me is a completely different thing.[33] One company had products that used fewer toxic chemicals, but no company has eliminated them from the manufacturing process. I went to a local independent shoe store and asked the clerk if the store carried any athletic shoes that were ethically made with minimal chemicals.[34] She told me that what I was looking for does not really exist because there is not a big enough market to support it. In other words, there are not enough people who actively care about where and how their shoes are made to justify making shoes ethically in terms of labor practices and without toxic chemicals. This is further evidence of an economic model perpetuated by the Domination System. One could buy dress or casual shoes made by artisans, but even those are harder to find. Athletic shoes, though, are not part of that niche. I ended up buying a pair that, according to further internet research, is one of the most durable running shoes available.[35] I hope someone invents athletic shoes made from natural materials and then pays people a living wage to produce

32. For many years, going shopping was "the thing" that I did when I didn't have to work. I had totally bought into the advertisers and marketing departments who told me that more stuff is what I needed to be happy. Now, shopping is done almost under duress because it often creates a conflict in my mind when I need to compromise my ethics just to buy socks (or any other item that is hard to find because it wasn't made in a sweatshop).

33. Vegans do not use animal products of any kind so vegan shoes wouldn't be leather for example but could be made with all manners of synthetic materials and chemicals.

34. Shoes have become a significant problem from a waste standpoint because of the materials used to make them. See: Albers, Canepa, and Miller, "Analyzing the Environmental Impact of Simple Shoes."

35. I've worn my Altra running shoes for well over a year now for everyday wear, working out, and running. They are showing some wear but still perfectly serviceable.

them. Surely that couldn't be that hard when one considers that humanity has gone to the moon amongst many other stunning achievements.

We can also become much more selective with our other purchases as well. Tech gadgets be they used as tools or toys are one such area. Our lives revolve these days around technology. Most of us see things like personal laptop computers, tablets, and smartphones as necessities for work and school. I am writing now using a laptop purchased from a national consumer electronics chain. We use them for entertainment and often become "screen zombies" staring glassy eyed at our gadgets any time there is a pause in activity or even when spending time with other people.[36] Technology can make a huge difference in our lives often for the better. Yet, due to the capitalist model and modern advertising, we generate a great deal of waste and perpetuate the flawed system by succumbing to the urge to buy the latest upgraded phone or other gadget, which these days seems to happen every week. If we took care of them as if we understood the true costs of their various manufacturing processes and used them until they ceased to function correctly, then fewer resources would need to be extracted from the Earth by poor people, including children under ten, working in conditions that I personally would be loath to put up with and certainly would never send a child into.[37] All of which happens now, just to make new versions of the same tool every few months so people get locked into a continuous cycle of spending money and keeping up with the Joneses, all to ensure that stockholders dividends go up and up and up. If I, or perhaps you, would be unwilling to do a task or would never consider sending our children to do it, why do we expect people in Africa or Bangladesh to do it, just so we can stand in line at midnight to buy the latest phone or tablet despite the fact that the one we already have works just fine.

The laptop I have now was purchased in 2014 and replaced one that I had purchased in 2009. A tech friend of mine said that I should replace it because it was over five years old when I took it to him to get it fixed. I bought a new one and kept the old one as a backup. It was painfully slow yet still functioned after two more years of sporadic use. Then I learned that replacing the operating system on it could increase its speed and restore its functionality so I had my friend change it to an open source (free to the public) operating system. He tested it once the new system was installed

36. I found myself doing this so much that I have started to leave my phone in the other room to break the habit.
37. Crawford, "Meet Dorsen, 8, Who Mines Cobalt."

and it worked fine. That seven-plus year-old laptop has now been given new life and donated to a Haitian student who is, I hope, using it to help further her or his studies.

Regardless of the intended or truly needed purchases that we are to make, we can do so with a great deal more mindfulness. David Holmgren expands on the familiar "3 R's" of reduce, reuse, recycle by adding two more "R's" to the list, refuse, and repair.[38] The first one is vitally important, for we as potential buyers have all the power. Should we *en masse* refuse to buy sweatshop made goods, chemically laced products, items that will not readily biodegrade, or any other item whose production is ecologically destructive or whose labor to make them was unfairly compensated, then we would fundamentally change the system and suddenly an enormous market is available to a company bold enough to provide items such as all natural athletic shoes, clothing, long lasting, repairable and upgradable tech devices or other items made by people being paid a living wage.

Planned obsolescence would also be greatly diminished with more mindful purchasing. This trick of the trade ensures that an item will have an intentionally short life span so that people are forced to buy say a washer and dryer more frequently than our grandparents did despite better technology being readily available. Clothing is mass produced with planned obsolescence in mind as well, hence the tendency for even heavy-duty work clothes to wear out quickly under normal use and for new t-shirts to last less than a year before starting to come unstitched. The consumer driven economic system as it stands now is predicated upon people continuously making new purchases. It's like we've all sold our souls to the company store in a new, less obvious way, driven by marketing campaigns and advertising that convince us that to feel good we have to spend money on some product that truthfully, we do not need and will not last long once we bought it to assuage some form of emptiness in our lives.

The second "R," to reduce consumption, would naturally be bolstered by recreating durable goods rather than disposable everything. Most people in America could easily withstand reducing their consumption without any detriment to their quality of life. Right after being told in the Bible that the love of money is the root of all evil, we are reminded that we should be content with having adequate food, clothing, and shelter. Despite the commercials on our screens trying to convince us otherwise, we cannot buy

---

38. David Holmgren, *Permaculture: Principles and Pathways*, 112.

our way to happiness. If that were possible, America would be the happiest place on Earth, which by most measures it most assuredly is not.[39]

Creative reuse is a wonderful idea that is put into practice by people smart enough to "waste not, want not." Americans throw perfectly usable items into the trash on a daily basis in a way that is mind boggling rather than finding a different purpose for it and then simply to replace it with something shiny and new. Artists and farmers are often good at reusing things. My wife, for example, loves to "upcycle" ordinary items that most would simply toss into the trash into works of art, or she will take a garment from a thrift store or from the back of her closet and recreate it into something new and exciting for her to wear. If people took into account, or even better, if it was made commonly known, the amount of energy that goes into making even the simplest of items---like bottle caps or packaging materials for instance, then perhaps reusing things would be a great deal more common. Many Americans used to have an ethic of reusing anything that could be reused or repurposed. This has since been lost in these days of planned obsolescence and online shopping. We had better find that ethic again and quickly before too much more perfectly usable stuff ends up in the already overcrowded landfills or shipped hundreds of miles to less populous regions.[40] Trash is never thrown "away"; it always goes somewhere.

Repairing items often goes hand in hand with reusing them. These days however, we are often told that it would be cheaper to replace something that is broke than to repair it. This is false economy. It may mean parting with fewer dollars from one's wallet, but it certainly costs a lot more in a holistic sense to mine the metals, refine the petroleum into plastics or fuel, transport all the materials required to a country with low labor costs, manufacture the consumer goods, and then ship it all to a wealthy country to be purchased. Meanwhile the broken item is most often discarded without the slightest regard to all mined metals inside the power cords and inner workings of tech gadgets and small appliances or without thinking about the people who slaved over a sewing machine for sixteen or more hours a day making a garment for someone to wear for a few months and then throw it away. The plastic found in so many things we buy, has become a pollutant of monumental proportions as is evidenced by the islands of visible plastic in the Pacific Ocean and the tiny unseen particles of it that aquatic life currently ingests, not to mention the ever-growing man-made

39. Hetter, "Where Are the World's Happiest Countries?"
40. Palmer, "Landfills: Are We Running out of Room for Our Garbage?"

mountains we call landfills. Further pollution of the oceans imperils us all. Building landfills and shipping garbage from place to place is unsustainable. We cannot put a truly fair price on the planet that supports us. It will take both individual action and systemic action via political movements and electoral processes to reverse this most asinine trend of destroying the planet and harming people for extremely short-term gain.

Recycling is the last "R" and should be our last resort because of the energy expenditure it takes to recycle glass, metal, plastic and paper.[41] Recycling is better than tossing things into the garbage because it does take less energy to recycle these items than to create new ones but, a lot of fossil fuel energy is used in the recycling process and in the case of paper, toxic chemicals as well. Disposable products should become the pariahs of the shopping public because they are a drain on resources, a strain on landfills, and a blight on communities in the form of litter. With paper, the initial manufacturing process needs to be changed from trees to hemp and the toxic bleaches that give us that crisp white paper should be outlawed as they are harmful to the environment. If those chemicals were not being used, then paper could be easily composted to create fertile soil instead of tossed in the trash.[42] Hemp grows exponentially faster than trees and therefore is far more renewable while also making great paper (in addition to many other useful things.)[43] Our forests could then be restored from monocropped species grown primarily for paper pulp or cheap lumber products to diverse forests teeming with life. The herbicides used on clear cuts to ensure that only commercially viable trees grow after the clear cutting takes place could then be eliminated thereby helping to keep in place the healthy soil and fungal networks that allow forests to thrive.[44]

As human beings, we are all connected and the choices we make when shopping for our needs and wants affects everyone within Earth's biosphere. Capitalism as a system needs a huge change in the systemic inputs in order to transform it into a system that works for the good of all humanity regardless of nation or ethnicity while maintaining the habitability of the planet and regenerating damaged systems as a matter of course.[45] As Americans, we have great purchasing power and it shows. With only five percent

41. Hutchinson, "Is Recycling Worth It?"
42. Schilgden, "Hey Mr. Green, Can You Compost Shredded Paper?"
43. Cholia, "The Top 5 Reasons Why We Should Grow Hemp."
44. See: Stamets' *Mycelium Running*.
45. Wink, *Naming the Powers*, 137.

of the global population, we generate thirty percent of the planet's waste, according to a study at the University of Utah.[46] That post-consumer waste damages the only planet we have to live on and hurts all our neighbors around the world. In a way, we are punishing the poor twice by supporting systems which exploit others for our pleasure and monetary gains, while also dumping the detritus of American life into the biosphere without any regard to the consequences. We can do better. We must do better in order to survive. We are called to do better by the Golden Rule and the command to love our neighbors; if we don't, we're going down with the ship. It's really that simple and there are already holes in the hull.

46. University of Utah, "How Much Do Americans Throw Away?"

4.

The Domestic Life
The Golden Rule at Home

OUR HOMES ARE MEANT to be places of sanctuary, where we escape from the pressures of postmodern life to be with our families, or for the introverted amongst us, to get much needed alone time. We recharge our batteries at home, yet we in wealthy nations can still virtually connect with the broader world via the internet and the TV in our pajamas or even in the buff if so desired. We also fill our refrigerators with food, kitchen cabinets with pots, pans, cookware, and kitchen gadgets; buy cleaning and grooming products; and fill our rooms with furniture; closets with clothing and shoes; and fill the entire house with stuff. Lots and lots of stuff. Home is where we eat, do our personal hygiene, and go to sleep most nights. It is the place we are to constantly improve, according to one big box purveyor of tools and building materials. In short, home is where, we hope, that the good stuff of life happens away from work, school, or running errands.

Our homes provide us with one of life's most basic necessities, shelter from the elements and the critters that run around at night. For many people, home comes complete with a plot of ground surrounded by grass and perhaps some flower gardens or shrubs and trees. Home should be a nice place for people to be. So, what does our home life have to do with the application of the Golden Rule, permaculture, or with loving our neighbors? How do the decisions we make regarding the cleaning and maintenance of our homes and yards, as well as the bathing and maintenance of our physical bodies within those homes, affect others? What can we as conscious people do to ensure that we are connecting meaningfully to our choices

35

so that we mindfully apply the Golden Rule to how we live in our homes? These thought-provoking questions will be the theme of this chapter and hopefully give us each some new-found knowledge which we can then apply with wisdom in order to better "do unto others as we would have them do unto us."

I was taught to do housework at what I consider to be an extremely young age. The first time I ever had to do the dishes I was only four years old. After having been given the most rudimentary instructions for how to proceed, I was told not to move from my stool at the sink until the seemingly mountainous pile of dishes was all done. I knew nothing of changing the water, adding more soap, or the best way to stack the dishes to dry. Later in life, I learned while in the Marines to make things clean enough to pass an absurdly over the top, make even the most obsessive cleaner happy, type of white glove inspection. That particular lesson came complete with a punch to the sternum from one of my more zealous, "old Corps" staff sergeants while in the Basic Heavy Equipment Operations Course at Camp Lejeune, NC in early 1991 when I failed to get the shower fixtures shiny enough, because heaven knows that shower fixtures must be shiny or the Earth may spin wildly off of its axis to the detriment of us all.

Cleaning the house is a chore that must be done, and to me the results are usually well worth it. A clean, uncluttered living space is generally a comfortable and relaxing place to be. Unfortunately, for most people, that clean house or apartment often comes at a huge price in terms of health and safety, as well as environmental damage due to the toxicity of many of the products on sale that make everything sparkle or smell "clean" and "fresh." I think that there is a tendency for people to assume that if a product is sold in a grocery store or other retail establishment that is must be safe to use. Alas, this assumption, as will be shown in the paragraphs following, is most definitely untrue. For everything from dish soap to laundry detergent, and from scouring powders to air fresheners, we are led to believe in "better living through chemistry" and urged to buy toxic products to clean, disinfect, and kill the perfidious germs that we're told lie in wait to sabotage our health and wellness all over every conceivable surface, especially in our kitchens and bathrooms.

According to the U.S. Bureau of Labor Statistics, Americans spent on average $660 on housekeeping supplies in 2016, of which $160 was on cleaning products and laundry supplies.[1] That is a significant chunk of change on products that are likely harmful to the environment. A great many of those items contain some sorts of fragrances which are often optimistically described as smelling like something wonderful from the natural world such as spring breezes, pine trees, or as one popular product slogan tells us to imagine as it gets sprayed liberally throughout the house, "odors out, freshness in." What exactly does freshness smell like anyway? To me these products actually smell like exactly what they are, chemicals concocted in a laboratory, and then sent to the marketing department for the purpose of convincing people otherwise. I can barely stand to walk down the aisle of cleaning products in a mainstream grocery store because the chemical smells are so overpowering they become a full-fledged assault on my olfactory senses. Perhaps I notice them so much because I never buy them anymore and almost always shop in stores that refuse to carry toxic products. A good deal of those noxious smells come from 'fragrances' of which one third are known to be toxic.[2] I would venture a guess that many more are toxic though are as yet unknown to be so. Some of the known toxic fragrances are even toxic if inhaled, which is precisely the purpose of a fragrance! That means there is an incredibly high probability that the stuff you are spraying into the air as air freshener, or pouring into the dispenser in the washing machine, into your sink or the toilet bowl, is a toxic substance that you then breathe the fumes of.

Remember that the next time you open your laundry detergent and get a whiff of whatever smell they're selling to you. Often these soaps and other cleaners with their combination of toxic ingredients (phosphates, fragrances, and antibacterial agents) are sent into the water treatment system to be treated with yet another noxious chemical – chlorine.[3] Not only that but buying and using these products can definitely put family members at risk for toxic exposure. The U.S. Poison Control Data from 2014 showed that 11% of all such toxic exposures come from cleaning supplies.[4] Are sparkly dishes or chemically laced laundry with faux nature smells worth the risk or poisoning ourselves, family members or our drinking water? Of

1. Wilson, "Consumer Spending on Household Cleaning Supplies," email message to author, February 9, 2018.

2. Organic Consumers Association, "How Toxic Are Your Household Cleaning Supplies?" See also: Science Daily "Toxic Chemicals Found in Common Scented Laundry Products."

3. Centers for Disease Control and Prevention, "Facts about Chlorine."

4. National Capital Poison Center, "Poison Statistics National Data 2016."

course not, yet we are duped into thinking that this is how to do things, in large measure because of the "trade secrets" loophole which allows companies to avoid fully disclosing their ingredients, as well as allowing them to "regulate" themselves.[5] This is another instance of the Domination System at work in our economic reality. Profits matter, people and the systems that foster life, do not and are actively worked against in the name of deregulation and higher profits.

Water will be a recurring topic throughout this chapter because so much of what we do at home involves water, and because water is literally the basis for *all* life.[6] The water on Earth's surface allowed for life to proliferate here. Humanity cannot survive without clean, potable water to drink, and that is in short supply due to pollution and the fact that less than 1% of the total water in the entire world is actually available for drinking (salt water and glaciers account for most of the Earth's water.)[7] The United Nations is urging water cooperation because it estimates that 783 million people globally do not have access to clean water.[8] That's over double the population of the United States, which now stands at approximately 323 million. Let that sink in for a second. That number is higher than the combined total populations of the U.S., Canada, and Mexico by 295 million people. It's higher than the entire population of Europe by about 40 million.[9] Yet we in the developed world treat water as if it were some sort of infinitely available commodity that can be abused at will, despite the fact that all the water that ever will be made has *already been made*. Once it's tainted with one of the 60,000 chemicals currently in use in the U.S.[10], how long will it be before the water will be is no longer safe to use?

The hydrologic cycle (how water moves through various phases of ice, precipitation, flowing water and its movement around the globe)[11] ensures that the water in your toilet bowl, sink, or shower will end up falling as rain or as drinking water on the other side of the planet at some point of the cycle, but not before it ends up in our own watersheds, thus imperiling both

5. Joseph, "Is 'Fragrance' Making Us Sick?"
6. Ghose, "Why Is Water So Essential for Life?"
7. National Academy of Sciences, "Where is the Earth's Water."
8. United Nations, "Water."
9. Imagine the furor if a nation of Anglo-Europeans lacked access to clean water rather than the large number of people of color in the global south who lack access to it.
10. Duhigg, "Millions Drink Tap Water That Is Legal, but Maybe Not Healthy."
11. NOAA, "Description of the Hydrologic Cycle."

our immediate neighbors and our global ones. Putting toxic chemicals in the water is definitely the opposite of "doing unto others as we would have them do unto us" and we're doing it on a daily basis to the detriment of ourselves, children, and humanity in general.

In May 2002, the U.S. Geological Survey found persistent detergent metabolites in 69% of all the streams tested and disinfectants in 66% of the tested streams.[12] We're robbing future generations of clean water in order to clean our homes, dishes, and clothing, and it's entirely unnecessary, idiotic, and is clearly not "loving our neighbors." Not to mention the inordinate amount of waste that comes from single use metal aerosol cans of disinfectants, shaving cream, and "air fresheners." Plants are the true air fresheners, chemicals are not, they only mask other smells. We can do a tremendous deal of good by refusing to buy such products. If we refuse to buy them, the companies that currently make them will either adjust or go bust. Almost anything that has a label proclaiming any of the following words: Caution, Warning, Danger, or Poison should be left on the shelf, and if known to be toxic, then banned outright immediately. When a product is suspected to have toxic ingredients, then those chemicals should be removed from all consumer products. When shopping, you can look for labels that say: No Solvents, No Phosphates, or for those made with plant based ingredients, and buy those instead if you want to avoid toxic products and potentially harming yourself, others and the environment. If you want fresher air indoors, fill your home and workspace with plants.[13]

The Environmental Working Group (EWG)[14] has an information-packed website that rates cleaning products based upon the types of ingredients that they contain. They also give lower ratings for products with undisclosed ingredients on the products' labels. Stick to their 'A' rated products to maintain your home in a far less toxic way, thus keeping you and your neighbors safe. Castile soaps from companies like Dr. Bronner's are excellent choices for dish soap and laundry detergent. The company uses fair trade and organic ingredients in its products and the fragrances they use are all natural (my personal favorite is their peppermint soap which is their best seller.)

---

12. Responsible Purchasing Network, "Cleaners: Social & Environmental."

13. Palermo, "Do Indoor Plants Really Clean the Air?"

14. For information on a variety of consumer products see: Environmental Working Group, "Consumer Guides."

For surface cleaning, it is better ecologically and cheaper to make some of your own cleaning solution, which is remarkably simple. Buy yourself some organic oranges (only use organic oranges as conventionally grown citrus fruits are sprayed with agricultural fungicides.)[15] Place the orange peels in a quart sized jar and pour in distilled white vinegar, preferably organic. Let it sit for two weeks and shake the contents three or four times during that period. The orange oil comes out of the peels and makes the mildly acidic vinegar an even better cleaning agent than it is by itself and it smells mildly of oranges. Pour the finished contents into a reusable spray bottle with 2/3 water and 1/3 of the orange peel – vinegar solution, and voilà, you have an inexpensive, highly effective cleaner for all the surfaces in your house including the toilet bowl. For scouring powder, it is tough to beat Bon Ami. Its ingredients are biodegradable and it contains no perfumes, dyes, or phosphates. Between that and the bottle of vinegar with orange oil that I made, our place gets clean enough to make even a drill instructor happy, at least before company arrives!

When Europeans first invaded North America, the local inhabitants were appalled by how terrible these newcomers smelled because the folks from Europe rarely bathed. For many Europeans of that era, bathing was an annual occurrence if it was done at all. The indigenous people, however, were far more fastidious about their hygiene and grooming. The Europeans, according to Charles C. Mann in his excellent book, *1491: New Revelations of the Americas before Columbus,* described the native inhabitants as strong, powerful people with little sickness or signs of ill health amongst them. Everything these first nations people used to groom and clean themselves was completely natural from the fresh, clean water that they bathed in, to the dyes they used, and the bear grease for oiling their hair. Folks of European descent and others finally caught on to the idea that bathing more than once a year is a good idea, yet the ways most folks go about grooming is far from natural these days. Like cleaning the house, our personal grooming can create unnecessary damage to our own health and to the health of the local ecological systems which surround us. Many soaps, shampoos, shaving creams, lotions, and toothpastes contain questionable ingredients and some ingredients that are already known to be toxic. As in the days when lead was heavily used in makeup for the European elite, people throughout society are still poisoning themselves in the name of vanity.

15. Adaskaveg, "Major Post-harvest Disease of California Citrus."

Part of the issue is that many of the ingredients remain a secret and are not listed on the products that are commonly sold. Fragrances are often toxic in grooming products as well as the aforementioned household cleaners but are not the only things we have to look out for. One such group of chemicals is called phthalates and is found in many products from plastics to grooming products. These chemicals have been linked to endocrine disruption, abnormal sexual development, birth defects, and retained insulin in males.[16] They can even be passed from expectant mothers to the womb, thus damaging the growing fetus and causing hormonal problems due to the effect on both testosterone and estrogen. Despite this well documented toxicity, some billion pounds of phthalates are produced each year, and they are generally found in the U.S. population in people's urine.[17] This isn't the only chemical problem with grooming products. There are vast numbers of chemicals lurking in them from the aforementioned fragrances to foaming agents, phosphates, heavy metals, and synthetic vitamins used in lotions and creams, all of which pose a risk to us and the environment.

Then there is triclosan, a chemical used as an antimicrobial to kill bacteria. This chemical has been prevalent[18] in many consumer products, especially hand cleaners and soaps, and is thought to be contributing to antibiotic resistant bacteria. It is also being found in water samples, human breast milk and blood plasma, earthworms, and even dolphins according to the National Resources Defense Council website.[19] The hazards of using it are many and yet its use is completely unnecessary, according to the FDA who says there is no evidence that using an antibacterial soap is more effective than using regular soap and water to stay clean. There is a growing body of evidence to suggest it is actually making us sicker. I once had a chiropractor tell me that if you cannot put it in your mouth to eat then you definitely shouldn't put it on your skin, which he told me is our largest organ. From a theological standpoint, this persistent pattern of creating, marketing, and selling products toxic to humans and our planet's ecosystems

16. Westervelt, "Chemical enemy number one: how bad are phthalates really?" See also: Endocrine Society, "Phthalate, environmental chemical is linked to higher rates of childhood obesity."

17. Centers for Disease Control and Prevention, "Phthalates Factsheet."

18. The FDA banned triclosan and other antibacterial agents in consumer products in 2016. They can still be used in hospitals and food service though. See: Kodjak, "FDA Bans 19 Chemicals Used in Antibacterial Soaps."

19. Greenfield, "The Dirt on Antibacterial Soaps."

is evil[20] and it is a sign that the system is in need of both a spiritual and a temporal overhaul.

Making a conscious choice requires research. The words "all natural" or any variation on the "natural" theme mean absolutely nothing, whether on a food item or a grooming product. Using "natural" is simply a marketing gimmick meant to fool shoppers into thinking that it is in fact sourced from nature and therefore safe and healthy to use. Some of the ostensibly eco-friendly, healthy products companies use ingredients that the Environmental Working Group (EWG) rates as highly hazardous to health or the environment. Making use of terms like "all natural" is often simply 'green washing' – an attempt to fool consumers into buying a product by making it sound environmentally friendly. The environmental pollution caused by these noxious chemicals is, and I cannot stress this enough, of vital importance to eliminate if we are to truly love our neighbors and do to them as we would do to ourselves. I have personally eliminated many of the products that I had bought in the past in an effort to conform to the absurd standards of a society that seems bent upon having vanity run amok like the people of "The Capital" in Suzanne Collins' dystopian series *The Hunger Games*. These days I use Dr. Bronner's almost exclusively for hand soap, bathing, and even as shaving cream (which I seldom need as I now have a quite unruly beard). Since I only shave once in a blue moon, I buy razors infrequently too which saves on both money and waste.

I stopped using conventional antiperspirant/deodorant sticks regularly several years ago and not once have I ever been told that I stink. Occasionally I will use a deodorant stone, made with natural mineral salt like potassium alum, if I am going to be engaging with the public in some way. If I want to get fancy, I might use a small amount of some essential oil, like clove or peppermint, in order to smell like something other than a human being. Neither of those things is harmful to me or to the environment. I also bathe less often than most people. To be sure, if I work out at the gym, go for a long walk, or do physical labor, especially when it is hot and humid, I will take a quick shower. If for some reason I do not get sweaty I may go for days without showering, though I will wash my face and hands of course and also do a quick clean of my armpits to keep them "fresh and clean." My wife is an administrative professional and works for a local non-profit organization. In the fall and winter, she showers about once per week and the rest of the time just uses a rag with Dr. Bronner's soap to "bathe" with. As

---

20. This is an example of how radical evil can be. See: Wink, *Engaging the Powers*, 65.

the label says, the only two cosmetics we need are sleep and Dr. Bronner's! By showering less often we save tremendous amount of water and energy.

For dental hygiene, we did research to find the best possible toothpaste that we could that would meet our needs for getting our teeth clean while also being safe for the environment. That means buying toothpaste free of ingredients like sodium lauryl sulphate,[21] preservatives, bleaches, and artificial colors or sweeteners. Most often we buy fluoride free toothpaste because of the concerns about fluoride on personal health, especially cognition, according to research done at Harvard University[22] and the Fluoride Action Network's[23] website. We've even managed to find locally made toothbrushes that have replaceable heads and handles made from recycled materials, thus saving energy and waste again.

Christina loves to dress nicely and get made up on the weekends and has found that even cosmetics can be purchased that are safe for the skin and the environment. She searches the internet for organic lipstick, eyeliner, and eyeshadow before buying cosmetics. So far, she has been delighted with the results, and I must say, she always looks amazing! Facial creams and lotions can also be found that harken back to the days when olive oil was used to keep the skin healthy and glistening or the hair shiny. With practice, some of these items can be made fairly easily at home from natural oils. A couple of years ago for Christmas, a friend of ours gave us some wonderful homemade lip balm that she had made that worked every bit as well as the Burt's Bees that we usually get at the store. We shop at a local, independent store[24] whose owner makes the facial cream that Christina uses, as well as other hygiene products that are carried there. We use organic coconut oil as hair oil too, she on her hair, and I on my beard when I want to tame it just a bit. It works a treat, is made of only one edible ingredient, and I like how it smells too. Of course, we could get really extreme and simply refuse to bathe at all and let our hair get matted ala John the Baptist, but I think it behooves us to stay clean and reasonably well groomed in this day and age.

21. The following report states that SLS is toxic to marine life: National Center for Biotechnology Information, "Human and Environmental Toxicity of Sodium Lauryl Sulfate (SLS)."

22. Choi, "Impact of Fluoride on Neurological Development in Children." See also: Choi, "Media Statement."

23. Fluoride Action Network, http://fluoridealert.org/.

24. Shopping locally benefits local economies far more than shopping at a corporate retailer. Not to mention the community connections and friendships one can make when shopping at a small, local retailer.

We're proving that it can be done in a more ecologically friendly, thus more neighborly, way.

Let us now take a look at the lawn, that pervasive carpet of hyper-fertilized, monocropped green that is the goal of so many Americans who have been sold on the ideal by various lawn and garden companies. Perhaps this unnatural ideal harkens back to the days of landed elites who kept manicured lawns and rigidly geometric gardens meant to impose some misguided idea of order upon the landscape. In the U.S., lawns as we know them today began to become much more prominent during the post-World War II housing boom that saw the rise of the American suburb in planned developments like Levittown to meet the needs of returning military personnel from overseas who found the cities too crowded for their liking. As automobiles became ever more accessible, it was easier for folks to move to these suburban neighborhoods and sometimes even whole new towns, and then commute to work in their shiny automobiles. With all that space, it seemed to make sense to have a yard and once that idea took off, so did the idea of having a perfectly manicured lawn maintained so as to ensure a boring monoculture of nearly identical blades of grass. This type of "perfection" is only possible with a host of fertilizers, herbicides, and other chemicals designed to kill everything deemed a detriment to that living carpet whether the soil and climate conditions are favorable for growing grass or not.[25]

From an ecological standpoint, "well-manicured" lawns of the type touted by companies like Scotts or TruGreen are an environmental disaster for a variety of reasons. In the natural world, diversity of species is the norm – from the soil, which when healthy is literally teeming with billions of living organisms, to the surface where myriad plants, animals, birds, insects and arachnids proliferate, among others too numerous to name. This diversity is an anathema to chemically based lawn care companies who exhort us to feed our lawns[26] as well as wage an unwinnable (yet profitable for lawn care companies) war on the so-called weeds, bugs, and grubs, in order to create what is a wholly unnatural ecosystem. Nowhere in nature do mono-

---

25. I lived in El Paso, TX for a couple of years, a place with an annual rainfall of about 8–9" and yet people still had lawns there. On Fort Bliss U.S. Army Base, we were instructed to maintain a well-manicured lawn in the officer's housing area where we lived despite the constant lack of rain and the fact that those types of grasses grow poorly in the desert ecosystem.

26. Fertilizer run-off is a huge source of pollution for our nation's watersheds. See: Pierce, "Nonpoint Source Pollution Education: Fertilizing the Lawn."

cultures exist, so why would we intentionally create a monoculture around our homes and use phenomenal amounts of polluting chemicals to do it?[27]

Americans use an inordinate amount of chemical fertilizers and various killing chemicals (herbicides, fungicides, and pesticides) on their lawns. The fertilizers are problematic because they are cannot be made without fossil fuels, which are of course finite resources that are seriously depleted already. They are also responsible for a great deal of pollution because much of what gets applied to the lawn does not actually get taken up by the roots, rather it runs off into the watershed (the local drainage area defined by geographical features and the flowing water within that area) or goes into the groundwater.[28] In either case it becomes a pollutant. In still waters such as ponds and lakes, excessive nitrogen from farming and lawn fertilizers in the water creates a situation called eutrophication. This is a condition in waterways where the biological oxygen demand gets too high and causes ecosystemic collapse of water-based species. In simpler language, all the fish, plants, crustaceans, and other life forms die in water where there is not enough oxygen to meet the needs of the lake or pond's residents. Americans use around ninety million pounds of fertilizer per year on lawns.[29] Ninety. Million. Pounds.

To prevent weeds, horrifically toxic chemical herbicides are used. The key ingredient in many broadleaf herbicides is a chemical called glyphosate, which is found in the popular product RoundUp amongst others. This is the same chemical used in agricultural applications as a desiccant before harvest and it is known to be toxic. The World Health Organization has called it a "probable carcinogen"[30] and its heavy use is causing health and environmental damage worldwide. Despite this, anyone with the required funds can go to a garden center and buy it by the gallon with no training, no oversight on how it gets used, and no attempt to inform the purchaser that the product is toxic, and then proceed to poison their little corner of the world. Like the fertilizers mentioned above, it also runs off and gets into the water supply according to the U.S. Geological Survey (USGS). The USGS

27. Ecosystems, whether naturally occurring or manmade, are far healthier and resilient with a diversity of species, especially diversity where various plants, animals, and fungi have symbiotic relationships. See: Guelph University, "Biodiversity Helps Protect Nature against Human Impacts."

28. Scientific American, "How Fertilizers Harm Earth More Than Help Your Lawn."

29. The Week, "Blades of Glory: America's Love Affair with the Lawn."

30. Cressey, "Widely Used Herbicide Linked to Cancer."

testing has found it in rainwater, surface water and the air.[31] This is the same herbicide mentioned previously in relation to GMO crops. Locally here in Lancaster County, PA where I live, a group of nursing mothers had their breast milk tested, and glyphosate was found in one out of twelve of the women's breast milk. The tragedy of this is that using this product is, like so many other chemicals, completely unnecessary and wholly imbecilic. Horticultural vinegar is a perfectly adequate herbicide if one wants to kill weeds without pulling them out of the ground.[32]

Many of those so called "weeds" that are annihilated by means of chemical warfare are actually incredibly useful plants. Three of the more common "weeds" are dandelions, plantain, and clover. All of these should be allowed to proliferate naturally in your yard. I use dandelions as an illustration of the permaculture maxim of "stacking functions," which means to incorporate elements into a permaculture design that perform more than one function. Dandelions do at least five good things when left alone. These include: aerating compacted soil with a deep taproot which creates healthier soil conditions, that tap root is medicinal as a diuretic and is used as a coffee substitute, the leaves of young dandelions are a delicious, highly nutritious salad green and even older greens can be eaten, the flowers are an excellent pollinator plant attracting bees to an area especially in early spring, the flowers smell nice and are also edible, and finally children love to blow the seeds into the wind and the world could use more of that sort of thing.

Clover is also an excellent pollinator plant and the flowers of white clover are also edible. As a child, I would sit on the ground munching clover flowers and watching the bees buzz from flower to flower. Clover is also a nitrogen fixing plant. Nitrogen fixers take atmospheric nitrogen from the air and, in a symbiotic relationship with certain organisms in the soil, accumulate the nitrogen into nodules on their roots.[33] When the plant is cut or dies completely, the nitrogen is released, thus fertilizing the soil naturally without any need for synthetic fertilizers. Plantain is also a medicinal and edible plant. It, like the dandelion, is nutrient dense and thus should be picked for salads rather than blasted with RoundUp. Before foraging for

31. Gillam, "U.S. Researchers Find Roundup Chemical in Water, Air."

32. I know a Pennsylvania Master Gardener here locally who only uses horticultural vinegar as an herbicide in her work.

33. Rhoades, "What Are Nitrogen Fixing Plants?" See also: Homestead Gardens, "List of Nitrogen Fixing Plants."

wild plants, it is wise to get a good book on edible plants and then learn a few plants well.[34] These three common plants are a good, safe place to start.

When in the suburbs during the spring and summer, it is a daily occurrence to hear someone fire up the lawn mower to cut their grass. Lawn mowers are obnoxiously loud machines that seriously disturb the peace. The loudness alone is enough to make me want to ban them in neighborhoods (along with leaf blowers.) Mowers have to be used more often because of recommendations about keeping the grass at a certain length (unnaturally, by the way) and because so much of the water used in America goes to watering lawns, creating further growth that needs cutting. According to the Environmental Protection Agency, household water use increases 2–4 times in the summer because people are watering their lawns so often, and people are using 30–70% of their water for outdoor uses, of which up to 50% is wasted due to evaporation or run-off.[35] NASA estimates that lawns in the United States now cover an area approximately the size of Texas.[36] Let that sink in for a second, because Texas is enormous, over 63,000 square miles worth of enormous, and all that lawn needs an awful lot of water, up to 900 liters per person per day.[37] That is a staggering amount of water used for something that provides almost nothing in return, and like the fertilizer, the water often runs off doing absolutely no material good. That is a staggering amount of land that could be put to far better use as well. Think of the potential food grown on even half that amount of land, and then go plant an organic garden if you have a lawn.

Ozone action days occur when ground level ozone exceeds certain limits due to air pollution and atmospheric conditions. We have these here in Southeastern Pennsylvania frequently during the hot and humid summer months. I once made the mistake of riding my mountain bike on a hot, ozone action day in El Paso, TX. Not long into the ride I was struggling for breath and it escalated quickly into what felt like an emergency situation. I can only imagine that what I experienced was similar to an asthma attack because it felt like my lungs were full of cotton balls that blocked me

34. Ensure that the edible plant guidebook you purchase covers plants from your local area and that it has color pictures, preferably of all the different life stages of the plant. For the Midwest and Mid-Atlantic region, I have found Samuel Thayer's books to be excellent. See: Thayer, "Our Books," http://www.foragersharvest.com/our-books.html.

35. Environmental Protection Agency, "When It's Hot."

36. Milesi, Elvige, and Dietz, "A Strategy for Mapping and Modeling the Ecological Effects of U.S. Lawns."

37. Wile, "The American Lawn Is Now the Largest Single Crop in the U.S."

from getting the required level of oxygen. It was a frightening experience brought on by air pollution. Lawn mowers emit a great deal of pollution, up to eleven times more than cars.[38] When there is an ozone action day we are supposed to refrain from using gas powered lawn and garden equipment because of the pollution they emit, which makes the ground level ozone worse. When we ignore those warnings, we put people sensitive to air pollution and ourselves at risk and all for something that is wholly wasteful and unnecessary. Emissions are only one part of the pollution problem from gasoline powered lawn equipment.[39]

An estimated seventeen million gallons of fuel are spilled annually during refueling.[40] Seventeen. Million. Gallons. Again, this is moronic given the amount of energy spent getting the gasoline and the wars fought to secure its supply. It's also completely unnecessary. A rotary mower without an engine will cut that grass just fine when properly maintained and do it without the obnoxious noise, emissions, or spills that take place with conventional mowers. Sure, they require a bit more physical work, but most of us could use more exercise.[41] Perhaps the exertion required to use an Amish style mower would encourage people to turn their yards into something far more functional, like a garden.

During World War II Americans were encouraged to grow "Victory Gardens" in order to prevent food shortages.[42] Millions of Americans did just that. Now, imagine if people realized that the need to do so is even more dire today due to peak oil, loss of farmland and top soil, chemical agriculture, and a complete disconnect from where our food comes from. Growing our own food can and does do a world of good. Converting a significant chunk of those 63,000 square miles of lawn to organic food production would eliminate wastes, lessen use of fossil fuels, water, and toxic chemicals, make our neighborhoods quieter, while promoting community and neighborly involvement. Diets could be vastly improved by introducing new healthful foods from the garden, and the increase in physical activity would improve overall health and wellness. Soil regeneration would take

---

38. Steele, "Cleaner: Air Gas Mower Pollution Facts." See also: Snider, "Gas Lawn Mowers Belch Pollution."

39. Banks, "National Emissions from Lawn and Garden Equipment."

40. Steele, "Cleaner Air: Gas Mower Pollution Facts."

41. There is an obesity epidemic in America that more exercise would help to alleviate. See: Gussone, "America's Obesity Epidemic Reaches Record High."

42. Modern Farmer," 12 Fantastic Victory Garden Posters."

place through appropriate methods such as composting all the plant-based food wastes, encouraging worms, and using nitrogen fixers instead of synthetic fertilizers. We can help our needy neighbors by sharing the surplus as well and all of these things make the planet more inhabitable, which is a fantastic way to "do unto others."

Various types of gardens can replace lawns. Even small spaces can grow an amazing amount of food as has been shown by many people, including self-described plant geek Eric Toensmeier, who grows a couple hundred different species on 1/10 of an acre in Massachusetts.[43] Eric's passion is perennial food plants because they require less energy and work than annuals while also increasing biological diversity.[44] Pollinator gardens are another excellent lawn substitute providing that the plants used are not treated with pesticides known to kill bees, like neonicotinoids.[45] I have a small pollinator garden in my front yard that is at most 100 square feet. Doing a quick inventory of that cultivated ecosystem recently, I discovered that there are over twenty species growing there. A small meadow-like lawn, with the aforementioned dandelions, plantain, and clover, can be mixed with wildflowers and other flowering plants to create a bee, butterfly, and wasp haven. Without these pollinators, we cannot eat, so it behooves us to do as much as we can to help them thrive. In areas such as the east coast that were once heavily forested, a forest garden can be created to mimic a woodland or forest, while providing an abundance of food, fuel, and diversity. All of these can be done organically and using the principles of permaculture design, which will be covered in a later chapter. These gardens can bring people together through conversation, sharing the surplus, and the sheer beauty of intentionally designed ecosystems.

The way we live in and maintain our homes and outdoor living spaces does not happen in isolation. Currently, it is happening within the context of the Domination System of the principalities and powers that run our capitalist system which reduces human beings and the biosphere to things.[46] Our actions, be they the purchases we make, the equipment we utilize, or the resources we use, all have an effect on our neighbors, both in our communities and farther afield. The amount of trash we generate too

43. Toensmeier, "Paradise Lot."

44. See Toensmeier's book on perennial vegetables here: http://www.perennialsolutions.org/organic-gardening-permaculture-book-perennial-vegetables.html

45. Dengler, "Neonicotinoid Pesticides Are Slowly Killing Bees."

46. Wink, *Naming the Powers*, 109.

affects others through resource use and the land required to dispose of it all. We like to throw things "away" without ever considering where they go or if these things could be useful to someone else. We are connected to our neighbors by the air we breathe and the water we need to survive as well as through technology, communities, and nation of origin. In the developed world, and in the United States in particular, as a society we are taking more than our share of resources for our hyper-consumptive lifestyles while being isolated from the people in our own neighborhoods. Often, we are blind to the effects our consumption has on our global neighbors. We can do better than this and would do better than this if we mindfully applied the Golden Rule to our homemaking activities, personal grooming, and how we maintain our little patch of Earth. What a great way to start loving our neighbors.

5.

Entering a Forbidden Zone
Politics

POLITICS IS USUALLY THOUGHT of as a subject best left well enough alone when one is at family gatherings, parties, the break room at work, and these days on social media platforms. Political discussions can be incredibly divisive and can inspire fanatical zeal on one end of the spectrum and complete apathy on the other. Politics concerns us here because at the national and state level, generally speaking, our political reality affects us and our neighbors. The candidates and the ballot initiatives we vote for can have a profound impact upon us and our neighbors, both locally and globally. At the risk of potentially alienating some folks for whom political party is sacrosanct, I must enter this largely forbidden and often contentious zone. I am, for purposes of transparency, an independent with Green Party leanings and a sincere desire for bioregional autonomy, for reasons which, if they are not apparent already, hopefully will become so by the end of this chapter. My intention here is to make my case for using the Golden Rule as the rubric by which people of faith or no faith at all can cast their ballots in order to create a more equal playing field for all of us, and especially those people who have been marginalized and disenfranchised by our political machinations in the past.

In my early twenties while in the Marines I was fairly apolitical, though we did have a discussion in my unit about President Bill Clinton's "Don't Ask, Don't Tell" policy when it was enacted. Today's version of me is appalled by the ignorance of my twenty-one-year-old self. For example, I had a hat made at the local mall as a result of that "Don't Ask, Don't Tell" discussion that said "I Support Gun Rights and Gay Control" because one of the sergeants had made that awful play on words as a joke and in my ignorance, I had thought it was clever. My personal evolution in that area, from ignorant, religiously based abhorrence, to compassionate, loving, and complete acceptance of LGBTQIA people, gives me hope that not only will I continue to grow in other areas to be a more Jesus like human being but that others will do likewise.

By the mid-90s my then father-in-law introduced me to hard core Republican politics in Alabama. Rush Limbaugh was constantly being played on his radio and CSPAN would invariably be on their TV at some point during the day. As a true Southern Baptist, he was ardently in favor of anything that Limbaugh and other right-wing ideologues had to say, as America was being "held hostage" by Bill Clinton and the baby killers.[1] I voted in a presidential election for the first time in 1996 and my father-in-law told me on the way to the polling station to vote the straight Republican ticket. So, like a sheep and without any critical thinking, that is exactly what I did and in so doing, I ended up voting for Jeff Sessions to be a Senator and Bob Dole for president. This trend continued during the 2000 election cycle when I voted Republican again, for George W. Bush in what turned out to be a disastrous election both at home and abroad. Then I voted for Republican Linda Lingle in Hawai'i's gubernatorial election a couple of years later and regretted it almost instantly as she immediately tried to accommodate more cars on Oahu's already overcrowded highways instead of creating a viable mass transit system for the nearly 1 million inhabitants of that tiny island. [2]

By 2004, my college education had begun to sink in and the conservative politics of my father-in-law and my now ex-wife no longer made any sense to me from an ethical, moral, or critically thought out standpoint. The more I learned about American history, the chemical warfare on the environment, social justice and human rights issues, and how to engage in critical thinking, the more liberal – or progressive-minded I became. This continues today, as I learn more about the social context of the prophets of the Hebrew Bible, first century Palestine, and the radically anti-imperial, pro-love, pro-equality teachings of the Galilean shaman called Jesus

1. If memory serves, this was the rhetoric Limbaugh used during Clinton's time as president. Mercifully, I have not listened to Mr. Limbaugh in years.
2. Dingeman, "Double-Decking Freeway among Lingle's Proposals."

of Nazareth who was executed by the Roman Empire for acts of sedition against the state.[3]

As I write this, the United States is enduring Donald Trump's rocky term as 45thPresident of the United States, after what was a truly a mind-boggling presidential election cycle, which was played out as the complicated, war torn tenure[4] of Barack Obama wound to a close. The rhetoric on the campaign trail was vitriolic hate speech from certain camps, like those of now President Donald Trump[5] and Texas Senator Ted Cruz[6], who seemingly wanted to drag the U.S. into an alt-right hell marked by white supremacy, the skewed religious values of Empire Christianity,[7] and total obeisance to corporate whims and authority. On the other side, Hillary Clinton was running as a Democrat while acting a lot like a Republican, as is evidenced by her positions on hydraulic fracturing (also known as fracking), genetically modified crops, warmongering, corporate handouts, and cushy ties to Wall Street banks who had no problem handing her large sums of money for making speeches to them. I find it hard to believe that she reprimanded those banks or warned them that there would be impending legal changes to the financial system to prevent further malfeasance if she became president while being paid $1.8 million to make speeches to them.[8]

Her presumed coronation as the nominee for the Democratic Party had a wrench thrown into the works by the lifelong activist and left leaning independent senator from Vermont, Bernie Sanders. His campaign energized millions of voters and resulted in angst and gamesmanship by the establishment of the Democratic Party elite because he opposes a great deal of what the ostensibly progressive Democrats stand for. He is also in favor of things that make laissez-faire capitalists and Ayn Rand devotees such as current House Speaker Paul Ryan cringe, such as a living wage for everyone, universal health care, higher education, and, real action on climate

---

3. Weaver, *The Nonviolent Atonement*, 42.

4. During Obama's last year in office alone, the U.S. dropped 26,171 bombs on people whose nations have literally no chance of invading the United States. See: Grandin, "Why Did the U.S. Drop 26,171 Bombs on the World Last Year?"

5. Kamp, "Donald Trump and the Escalation of Hate."

6. Saletan, "Ted Cruz's Shameful Attempts to Blur the Line between Muslims and Islamic Extremists."

7. Weaver, *The Nonviolent Atonement*, 83. See also: Zahnd, *A Farewell to Mars*, 33–50.

8. She says making the speeches was a mistake given the climate around the banking industry after 2008–9. See: Epstein, "Clinton Says Giving Paid Speeches to Wall Street Firms a Mistake."

change. Ironically, because he is neither a practicing Jew nor Christian, it was only in his campaign speeches and answers to political pundits' questions about his faith that the topic of the Golden Rule, which he asserts "is not very complicated,"[9] ever came up.

As voters, we are supposedly the ones with the power to make positive changes in the course of the nation in terms of policy both domestic and foreign, yet most often we fail to do so. For the entirety of the history of the United States of America, the leaders and the voters have let down and disenfranchised countless people because of ignorance, intolerance, or a false sense of superiority, both racial and religious. From the beginning, when only white, land owning males could vote and African slaves were considered subhuman (being counted as three-fifths of a person in census data)[10] until today, various groups are still reviled or made into scapegoats, such as people of color, primarily black people and immigrants, along with Muslims and other non-Christian religious groups, and gay, lesbian, bisexual, transgendered, intersexed, and asexual (LGBTQ) people. These scapegoated people, all of whom are our neighbors as defined by Jesus, are discriminated against systemically by the elected representatives of both parties, but most often the Republican Party,[11] as evidenced by the many oppressive policies they put forth and the rhetoric that comes from too many Republican politicians.[12] They continue in their roles, being enabled

9. Corasaniti, "Bernie Sanders Makes Rare Appeal to Evangelicals at Liberty University."

10. The roots of today's vitally important Black Lives Matter movement are deep. The so called three-fifths compromise is one of those roots. See: Laws.com, "Three Fifths Compromise."

11. A quick internet search about repressive policies put forth by the Republican Party and its elected members can be revelatory. Legislation to deny members of the LGBTQIA community human rights, denying women agency over their bodies, and blatantly racist policies towards blacks and other people of color are usually Republican initiatives. As a current example, see how many Republican politicians and pundits said that Colin Kaepernick's decision to kneel during the anthem was disrespectful to the anthem and to military people, despite the fact that it had nothing to do with either. It has always been about systemic racism perpetuated by police and public policies that unfairly target black people. As one example see: Applewhite, "Enough Talk: Republicans Must Walk the Walk on Systemic Racism." See also: Mazza, "Several Eagles Players Already Planning to Skip White House Visit."

12. Near Chicago, a former Nazi party member and holocaust denier is on the ballot running for Congress. The Republican Party did nothing to distance themselves from him. See: Kranz, "A Holocaust Denier and Former Nazi Party Leader is Poised to Become the Republican Nominee for Congress in Illinois

by the people who vote for them, many of whom identify as Christians. Their collective legislative actions, words, and choice of candidates, shows that they have an incredibly poor understanding of the religion they claim to follow with its emphasis on nonjudgment, love of enemy, love and care for neighbors, and nonviolence. Democratic Party politicians also have much to answer for in terms of perpetuating human rights abuses, systemic racism, mass incarceration, and imperialism maintained by advanced weaponry.

The rhetoric of the far-right spouts bigotry and hatred in the name of free speech.[13] There has been a huge increase in incendiary rhetoric and racist extremism since Donald Trump first rose to the nomination as the Republican candidate for president, and even more so once he became president.[14] During Trump's campaign there were acts of violence at his campaign rallies committed by both opponents and supporters, some of the incidents were clearly racially motivated against black opponents of then candidate Trump.[15] A Trump presidency was frightening for millions of people to contemplate given his blatant racism, bringing forth visions of race riots all over the country, religious zealots and white supremacists coming out of the woodwork wreaking havoc and violence upon their neighbors while setting the nation back a couple hundred years in terms of human rights and environmental policy. Sadly, some of those visions have turned out to be prophetic since Trump's inauguration as he and his cabinet have begun dismantling the Environmental Protection Agency's regulations in favor of profit mongering chemical and fossil fuel corporations,[16] A Muslim ban put forth by the president has been rejected multiple times by higher courts,[17] ICE agents are deporting immigrants in droves which is sparking panic in immigrant communities,[18] and Cold War era saber rattling has been replaced by two attention seeking authoritarians, Donald Trump and North Korea's leader Kim Jong Un, threatening nuclear war

13. Given, "Milo Yiannopoulos and Richard Spencer Remind Us What Free Speech Is and Isn't."

14. Potok, "The Year in Hate and Extremism."

15. Mathis-Lilley, "A Continually Growing List of Violent Incidents at Trump Events."

16. Trump's first pick to run the E.P.A., Scott Pruitt, is a former insider who sued the E.P.A. multiple times. See: Worland, "Scott Pruitt's Mission to Remake the EPA."

17. Dolan and Kaleem, "U.S. 9th Circuit Court of Appeals Refuses to Reinstate Trump's Travel Ban."

18. Riley, "What to Know About Recent Immigration Raids in U.S. Cities."

which is making citizens and politicians nervous.[19] Every day seems to bring a new horror for the marginalized.

The election cycle that brought us a Trump presidency proved that the "fix is in." Electoral fraud, voter suppression, and media blackouts have all taken place in broad daylight as it were. The surprising aspect, if there was one, was that this had mostly come from the Democratic side of the aisle and by what has often been optimistically described as "the liberal media." It was all brazenly done. Every idiotic, bigoted, sexist, xenophobic comment or his calls for violence that Trump uttered were blared all over the various 24-hour news channels, while Sanders' campaign and the millions voting for him were largely ignored for much of the primary season.[20] Debbie Wasserman Schultz, then chairwoman of the Democratic Party, came out and said point blank that the system was rigged for the establishment. During an interview on a mainstream news program, she noted that the party's superdelegates existed to ensure that grassroots candidates like Senator Sanders would get weeded out and have no chance to win.[21] Like the Republicans, the Democratic Party knows who its major donors are—the same corporate lobbyists and Super PACS that donate to the Republicans. The Democratic Party bows down to them obsequiously in like manner. That is why the establishment keeps moving to the right as both parties seek to consolidate power, while the citizenry is actually moving to the left and wants more progressive policies,[22] many of which when enacted would show a measure of concern for "the least of these," our marginalized neighbors.

This move to the right by the established political "authorities" is why fracking is legal and RoundUp is being sprayed in frightening amounts all over public and private land. It is why Kansas[23] and Louisiana[24] are in economic trouble due to Republican tax cuts, and why Alabama, in an effort

19. Tharoor, "Trump's Saber-Rattling at North Korea Sparks Fears."

20. Democracy Now!, "Bernie Blackout?"

21. Norton, "Un-Democratic Party."

22. Court documents affirm that the DNC did rig the primary in favor of Clinton. Sanders likely would have beaten Trump in a landslide. See: Curl, "Court Concedes DNC, Wasserman Schultz Rigged Primaries for Hillary." See also: Rifai, "Sanders has Potential to Beat Trump."

23. Rushe, "Kansas's Ravaged Economy a Cautionary Tale." See also: Berman, "Kansas Republicans Sour on Their Tax-Cut Experiment." And: Mazerov, "Kansas' Tax Cut Experience Refutes Economic Growth Predictions."

24. Grace, "How Bobby Jindal Broke the Louisiana Economy."

to suppress the black vote, closed a large number of driver's license offices, all of which happened to be in towns where mostly black people would need to use them to get the required state ID in order to vote.[25] It's why systemic racism is still so prevalent in America today.[26] It is also why the U.S. military budget (more on this in chapter six) is disproportionately large, despite the fact that the continental U.S. has not been invaded by a foreign nation since 1812, and why war profiteers continue to enrich themselves[27] using the men and women of the armed forces as disposable people. "Our" foreign "enemies" become target practice and fodder for bombs while civilians killed by the thousands are deemed "collateral damage." In short, this is exactly what an oligarchy looks like and that is what a recent Princeton University study concluded that the United States in fact is.[28] An oligarchy serves only a small number of people while treating the rest of us as less worthy of human rights, decency, and basic needs than the self-styled elites. Donald Trump is overtly attempting to be the Oligarch in Chief with an authoritarian slant apparently modeled on his buddy Vladimir Putin and others of his ilk. This type of system and behavior is the polar opposite of doing unto others as we would have them do unto us.

How did we get to this point? How have we come so far from the national narrative of being a beacon of freedom, the "shining city on the hill," a land where all people are created equal? National "leaders" insist that this narrative is still in effect, when in point of fact, it never actually has been even remotely true. They say the patriotic sounding words, wear the flags on their lapels, but it is all empty, meaningless, horse hockey. Please forgive the expression, I can think of no better one to describe the festering, malodorous stench that emanates from the so – called halls of power. They make little or no effort to try to hide the malfeasance any more. Answering the question of how this came to be is a complicated matter that could fill whole volumes. In broad terms however, I think it is reasonable to say that we collectively got here because the foundation the nation was built upon was highly suspect to begin with, and from that suspect foundation we have continued to build upon it until today, when it is starting to crumble in

25. Williams, "Democrats say Alabama's Closure." See also: Berman, "Alabama, Birthplace of the Voting Rights Act."

26. Nesbit, "America, Racial Bias Does Exist."

27. Defense industry contracts make millions of dollars for stockholders. Hartung, "Trump Is on His Way to Record-Setting Defense Spending in 2018."

28. BBC, "Study: U.S. is an Oligarchy, Not a Democracy." See also: Gilens and Page, "Testing Theories of American Politics."

earnest. Once again, we see the principalities and powers at work. Again, these principalities and powers are, "a generic category referring to the determining forces of physical, psychic, and social existence. These powers usually consist of an outer manifestation and an inner spirituality or interiority. Power must be incarnate, institutionalized or systemic in order to be effective. It has a dual aspect, possessing both an outer, visible form (constitutions, judges, police, leaders, office complexes), and inner invisible spirit that provides it legitimacy, compliance credibility and clout."[29]

The suspect foundation that I am talking about is made of the following bricks: false notions of racial/ethnic superiority, empire Christianity, slavery, murder, genocide, systemic patriarchal misogyny, militarism, and greed. For a good number of people this last sentence is perhaps new information. For others it may well be sacrilege. It is nevertheless true as the historical record indicates[30] and as further paragraphs will further briefly explain. The truth of these facts does not mean that nothing good or of value has ever come from the formation of these United States, though it does mean that we need to take a long, hard look at ourselves as individuals and as a nation in order to fully acknowledge the nation's past in all its horrific ugliness as well as the current national crisis that has exposed every national sin to the light and tarnished the U.S.' reputation globally. By acknowledging, rather than ignoring or glossing over this past, we can begin to heal the wounds that have been caused to so many millions of people. We must name the powers, unmask them, and nonviolently engage them in order to change both the system and the citizens that make it up.[31]

Anglo-European invaders[32] came to these shores with the idea of European exceptionalism firmly rooted in their minds. I use the term invaders rather than colonists because it is the correct one. To call them colonists gives them primacy and suggests that the millions of previous inhabitants of the Americas were less worthy of the land they had lived on for millennia than the Europeans who invaded. The religion that many of these invaders espoused was a form of Empire Christianity (the conflation of the church with the ruling secular authorities of the Roman Empire) largely devoid of

29. Walter Wink, *Unmasking the Powers*, 4.

30. For more in-depth analysis see: Zinn and Arnove, *A People's History of the United States*; Brown, *Bury My Heart at Wounded Knee*; Cone, *The Cross and the Lynching Tree*.

31. See Walter Wink's treatment of the powers in his three books on the subject, noted elsewhere in the bibliography.

32. 31 For more on Pre-Columbian history of the Americas, see: Mann, 1491.

the actual teachings of Jesus of Nazareth, while being heavy on violence, the divine rights of kings, patriarchy and an unholy lust for wealth. It completely ignored the parable of the Good Samaritan, Jesus' teachings about the poor and marginalized and peaceful yet proactive resistance, and replaced it with a God who took sides with the powerful and essentially gave them carte blanche to do whatever they wanted to do, so long as it was "in the name of God."

Consider Christopher Columbus, the devout Catholic explorer who, despite being profoundly lost, found some islands peopled with generous, placid, docile people and then decided to commit or condone wanton acts of cruelty including rape, torture, murder, and dismemberment of human beings who had been nothing but kind to him and his men. Greed and a lust for gold and glory drove Columbus and his men to commit these evil acts that resulted in genocide.[33] Yet we still have a national holiday honoring this man and a nationwide organization that lauds his exploits called The Knights of Columbus, which maintains a museum in New Haven, CT that holds him up as a hero. Honoring Columbus and those of his ilk is an abject racist insult to Native Americans and other indigenous people worldwide, for doing so proclaims an acceptance of his actions and the false notion that those he killed, maimed, raped and tortured "had it coming" because they were "less than human" and believed the wrong things about divinity, how to be civilized, and how to take care of the land. Do you know anyone who actually wants to be treated as subhuman or have their ethnicity and traditional connection to the land and their Creator belittled? Of course not. Why then do we continue to sanction this type of foundational brick?

Cotton Mather is another example (there are numerous others) of the aforementioned faulty foundational bricks. His religious zealotry stemmed from his adherence to the Puritans' particular doctrine of the Christian faith. In his writings he used language that would be classified as hate speech today when describing Native Americans in Massachusetts. He referred to Indians as "savages," "furious tawnies," "oppressors," "idolaters," "raging dragons," and "devils."[34] To him, the indigenous inhabitants were agents of evil in league with the devil. After a massacre of Pequot Indians, who were burned alive by the misguided "Christians," Mather rejoiced saying that, "on this day we have sent 600 heathen souls to hell."[35] It is difficult for me

33. Zinn and Arnove, *A People's History*, 1–21.
34. "Sinful Sermon?"
35. Zinn and Arnove, *A People's History*, 15.

to imagine a less Christ like sentiment than that. Mather did not limit his hatred to Indians. He was also a key instigator of the misogynistic Salem witch trials and the hysteria that ensued as a result. Columbus, Mather, and those like them were men of their time and it is important to remember that. It is also important to tell their stories correctly in order to ensure that their legacy of bigotry, hatred, and misogyny can be repudiated and overturned at all levels of civil society. Until we do that, systems of oppression will remain in place, and many people will continue to suffer as a result.

America's shoddy foundation continued to be laid as the invaders' colonies grew and as governments began to be formed. Many of the statesmen who were later to become famous white men were slave owners.[36] One of our most famous and oft honored historical figures was not only a slave owner but a known rapist. Thomas Jefferson, second U.S. president, eloquent writer of the Declaration of Independence, the face on the two-dollar bill and the nickel, raped at least one of his slaves, Sally Hemings, and fathered as many as six children by her. A slave woman was not at liberty to give Jefferson consent to have sex. She was slave; he was master and could in those terms demand sex from her. Non-consensual sex is *always* rape.[37] He perhaps felt justified in his treatment of Hemings because Jefferson believed that blacks were "mentally inferior" to whites[38] and that a biracial society was impossible in America.[39] His views were common in those days and sadly for many remain so today. This foundational brick, as I call them should be labeled "systemic racism." Despite its inherent ugliness, this part of Jefferson's story should be told, for it will help to bring healing when acknowledged that so many problems in America have their roots in systemic racism. There are far too many people who deny the existence of systemic racism in America even today despite the preponderance of evidence that speaks to its existence.[40] The Powers continue to actively promote institutionalized racism as we have seen earlier in reference to

36. For a fascinating social history of enslaved people in America see: Davis, *In the Shadow of Liberty.*

37. Danielle, "Perspective | Sally Hemings Wasn't Thomas Jefferson's Mistress. She Was His Property." See also: Renegade, "No, Thomas Jefferson and Sally Hemings Did Not Have a Relationship."

38. Gordon-Reed, "The Jefferson Enigma – Blacks and the Founding Father."

39. The History Channel, "Sally Hemings."

40. A quick internet search will reveal sites and videos proclaiming that systemic racism does not exist or is a myth.

Alabama closing driver's license offices used primarily by black people, to cite just one example.

Jefferson was surely not the only slave owner to rape slaves. Depriving someone of freedom is an atrocity and an abuse of human rights. It creates a dynamic where people can be forced into unwanted sexual encounters, beaten, torn from their family, worked to death, and denied the most basic of human needs. Sadly, the practice of slavery is all too alive and well in the world today and still occurs even within the United States. The Global Slavery Index estimated in 2016, that over forty million people are held in slavery worldwide with 57,700 of those people in the United States alone[41] with many of those trafficked in the U.S. forced into unpaid prostitution. Slaves globally are forced to work on farms and shrimp boats, in mines and cacao plantations, and as sex workers among other things. Global slavery is not based upon race the way slavery in the United States became to be after the period when indentured servants were the prevalent type of free labor used. When politicians bow down to the Golden Calf, and citizens fail to recognize where the things they buy come from, it creates a system where slavery is seen as a means to increasing wealth. In order to engage in Neighbor Care, we must create the political will to change this system of oppression.

The Three-Fifths Compromise firmly established systemic racism as policy in the U.S. on July 12, 1787 when it was enacted. This compromise was put into effect to artificially limit the population of the Southern states to lower the number of Southern delegates to Congress.[42] In an ironic twist, the Southerners who owned the majority of the slaves in the Colonies wanted to count slaves the same way as whites were counted even though they believed that blacks were inferior. This would have given them a majority of representatives and helped to further the cause of slave owners who got rich off the backs of brutal unpaid, forced labor. The Three-Fifths Compromise made slaves subhuman legislatively and still gave the South undue political representation in Congress, for the blacks had no actual say in legislative matters despite being unwittingly used as political pawns as well as slaves.

41. Global Slavery Index, "United States – Prevalence." See also: Global Slavery Index, ""Unravelling the Numbers."

42. Laws.com, "What was the Three-Fifths Compromise?"

Systemic racism manifests itself in politics and public policy all of the time[43] and has since the earliest days of American "colonialism." This is a huge topic, so I will give only a few examples. Sadly, there are millions more as individual people of color get targeted on a daily basis throughout the nation simply because of the color of their skin. A further example from the 19th century is the Dred Scott case. Scott, a slave, had lived in territories where slavery was prohibited by law, as well as in slave holding Missouri. He sued for his freedom on the basis of having lived in a free territory and claiming citizenship there once his owner had died. The case went to the U.S. Supreme Court which ruled that Scott as a black man had *no rights of citizenship*[44] and that the government could not deprive someone of their property. This ensured that Scott and all other blacks, in the eyes of many were considered less than human and no more than property. The Dred Scott case was one of the final straws preceding the Civil War, which was fought by the South primarily to preserve slavery, according to Colonel Ty Seidule, head of the History Department at West Point, who claims that the Articles of Secession written by each seceding state declared that it was seceding to preserve slavery within its borders.[45]

In the twentieth and twenty-first centuries this pattern has continued. Voter suppression tactics based upon racial lines have been put into effect to deny blacks and Latinos the right to vote. Sometimes literacy tests[46] were devised to disenfranchise black voters, some of them were impossible for anyone to pass.[47] In recent years, there has been a push in many states for so called "Voter ID Laws" that claim to be about voter fraud but are really about preventing minorities from voting.[48] It is a divide and conquer tactic because people of color often vote for more progressive candidates who have the potential to upset the status quo. Many poor people cannot afford the fees that are charged when getting a state ID or they live too far away

43. Hobgood, *Dismantling Privilege*, 36. Quoted in: Kujawa-Holbrook, "Love and Power: Antiracist Pastoral Care," ed. Sheryl A. Kujawa-Holbrook and Karen B. Montagno, in *Injustice and the Care of Souls*, 21.

44. Zinn and Arnove, *A People's History*, 187, 198.

45. Seidule, "Was the Civil War About Slavery?"

46. See: Veterans of the Civil Rights Movement, "Voting Rights Are You 'Qualified.'"

47. Onion, "Take the Impossible Literacy Test."

48. Multiple states have had such laws overturned because the court ruled they were enacted to suppress minority votes. See: Malewitz, "Texas Voter ID Law Violates Voting Rights Act." See also: Associated Press, "Court Rules North Carolina Voter ID Law Unconstitutional."

from a place where they can go to get one, and public transit is either poor or nonexistent. Another voter suppression tactic is the use of gerrymandering in which political district lines are redrawn to ensure favorable results for incumbents or a certain political party, often by diminishing the size of districts where mostly minority voters live.

Systemic racism is also seen in the criminal justice system where blacks and Spanish speaking peoples are disproportionately targeted by law enforcement or receive sentences far harsher than those given to white people. Consider the fact that white people use drugs at the same rates as do blacks and Latinos, yet blacks are arrested at almost three times a higher rate than whites according to Human Rights Watch[49] and are sentenced to much longer jail time (19.1% longer)[50] as well. One of the roots of this particular branch of systemic racism goes back to the early days of marijuana prohibition where racism and xenophobia were stoked to get the once legal plant, which was known even then to have long history of medical uses, demonized to the point of its total prohibition. The propaganda surrounding marijuana was blatantly racist and xenophobic and played on the fears of white Americans.[51] Later, President Nixon, an avowed racist and anti-Semite,[52] intentionally started the so called "War on Drugs" in order to target blacks and the pro-peace movement. Nixon's chief domestic advisor John Ehrlichman said in a 1994 interview after his time in prison:

> The Nixon campaign in 1968, and the Nixon White House after that, had two enemies: the antiwar left and black people. You understand what I'm saying? We knew we couldn't make it illegal to be either against the war or black, but by getting the public to associate the hippies with marijuana and blacks with heroin, and then criminalizing both heavily, we could disrupt those communities. We could arrest their leaders, raid their homes, break up their meetings, and vilify them night after night on the evening news. Did we know we were lying about the drugs? Of course, we did.[53]

49. Human Rights Watch, "U.S: Drug Arrests Skewed by Race." See also: "Marijuana Arrests Are Rising and Police Target Blacks over Other Groups." And: Williams, "Marijuana Arrests Outnumber Those for Violent Crimes."

50. King, "Black Men Get Longer Prison Sentences." In Florida, blacks fare even worse, especially when sentenced by a white judge. See: The New York Times, "Unequal Sentences for Blacks and Whites."

51. McDonald, "The Racist Roots of Marijuana Prohibition."

52. Stein, "New Nixon Tapes Reveal Anti-Semitic, Racist Remarks."

53. LoBianco, "Report: Nixon's War on Drugs Targeted Black People."

Vilify. Target. Control. These are the tactics of the Domination System, which is antithetical to permaculture, the Golden Rule, and the love of neighbor.

This kind of "law enforcement" leads to racial profiling where it can become dangerous for a black person to do normal things like walk down the street or drive a car, which has spawned a bitterly ironic meme "driving while black," because black people are far more likely to be targeted than white people, simply for going about their daily business. On one end of the spectrum this leads to "stop and frisk" protocols where people of color are unlawfully searched simply for being out in public such as in New York City where over 80 percent of the people who were illegally searched were either black or Latino, according to the New York Civil Liberties Union, with some years as high eighty-seven percent.[54] Let that sink in for a second. This is *not* about law enforcement; it's about racism pure and simple.

On the other end it leads to the inordinate number of young black people beaten or even murdered by police which has led to riots and de facto militarized zones in some U.S. cities. Police departments circle the wagons and insist there was no wrongdoing despite the overwhelming evidence to the contrary. Recently, two more murders committed by police officers have taken place when Alton Sterling was shot and killed by police in Baton Rouge, LA and Philando Castile was killed during a routine traffic stop in Minnesota for being a black man with a licensed weapon.[55] Fred Hampton, Mumia Abu-Jamal, Rodney King, Trayvon Martin, and many others have been victims of this heinous type of enforced racism. If you don't know these names, please look them up and then stand up for the countless number of people like them, because doing so is a huge part of following the Golden Rule. One simply cannot be neutral in matters of injustice if one is not to be complicit in perpetuating further injustice.

Conservatives are often called out, and rightly so, for perpetuating systemic racism in favor of more egalitarian policies that actually support the notion that "all people are created equal." Democrats too share a significant portion of the blame. Bill Clinton's presidency, for instance, saw a huge increase in incarceration rates of blacks because he wanted to be

54. New York Civil Liberties Union, "Stop-and-Frisk Data."

55. Ordinarily the National Rifle Association loudly defends licensed gun owners, yet were strangely silent when Mr. Castile was murdered after telling the police officer he was licensed to carry and had a gun in the car. See: Selk, "Gun Owners Are Outraged by the Philando Castile Case."

seen as "tough on crime,"[56] which, like the phrase "War on Drugs," is code for "tough on the poor, the black, and the brown." Hillary Clinton during this period once referred to black offenders as "super predators" with "no empathy."[57] Like the Colonial Era, when Northern leaders who created the Three-Fifths Compromise, modern ostensibly progressive, faux liberal politicians often compromise far too much with those on the Right and then the "tranquilizing drug of gradualism" takes over, to borrow a phrase from the late, iconic civil rights leader Dr. Martin Luther King, Jr.[58]

America incarcerates a higher percentage of its population than any other nation.[59] Let that sink in for a second. The self-styled "Land of the Free" is throwing people into jail or prison at an unprecedented level that not even dictatorships achieve, and that was long before the want-to-be dictator Donald Trump took office. More and more, prisons are now for-profit enterprises and carry on the legacy of the "convict leasing program" made possible by the 13th Amendment and utilized by rich people to get even richer by using unpaid convict labor.[60] Because they idolize money and power, right-wing politicians, support these for-profit prisons.[61] Given even a moment's thought, for-profit prisons should be a complete non-starter given the blatantly obvious potential for abuse. A for-profit prison cannot make a profit without prisoners. Making laws more racially equal by ending the War on Drugs, stop and frisk patrols, the arrest of immigrants, and racial profiling would seriously jeopardize those profits. One solution would be to ban for-profit prisons and vote out any politician who supports them, because obviously they care more about money than freedom, human rights, and racial equality.

Systemic racism is also perpetuated through educational policy. Schools and the students they serve are caught in a perpetual cycle of underachievement, poverty, and the crime that accompanies them because education dollars are largely based upon property taxes.[62] How on earth do we expect kids in poor neighborhoods to reach their potential as a matter

56. Norton, "Bill Clinton Continues to Defend."
57. Norton, "Bill Clinton Continues to Defend."
58. King, "I Have A Dream."
59. American Psychological Association, "Incarceration Nation."
60. Douglas-Bowers, "Slavery by Another Name."
61. Hamilton, "How Private Prisons Are Profiting."
62. Turner, Khrais, and Lloyd, "Why America's Schools Have a Money Problem." See also: Berry, "Property Taxes & Public Education Funding: Inequality in the System," 3.

of course, rather than the random anomalous child who rises above it all, when their schools are perpetually underfunded and poorly staffed? Kids in impoverished school districts lack even textbooks and the most basic of supplies,[63] yet we expect them to "pull themselves up by their bootstraps." It's patently absurd. Many people evince casual or overt racism when they blame the people in those neighborhoods, towns, and cities for their problems by saying things like, "they're just lazy" or "they're more prone to be criminals." We need to find a different, more equal way to distribute educational funding so that everyone, regardless of zipcode, ethnicity, economic background, or skin color, can have an environment conducive to learning in the learning style that best meets their needs (e.g., auditory, visual, kinesthetic).[64] How many potential geniuses have we as a society missed out on simply because the deck has been so firmly, deeply stacked against people of color specifically and poor people in general? More to the point, how many human lives have been tossed out as if meaningless simply because of the zip codes they lived in? These people are all our neighbors.

Banks have used a technique known as redlining that in a similar way perpetuates poverty. Redlining is to banking what gerrymandering is to voting. Put a redline on a map and deny mortgages to anyone who wants to buy a house within those lines or deny a loan to someone who currently lives within them and wants to move. Not surprisingly, those redlines are most often drawn around areas where people of color live. If loans are given, banks have been known to charge higher fees and interest to people of color, which again limits their chances at bettering themselves economically while enriching the banks. These toxic mortgages[65] lock people in a cycle of perpetual debt not unlike the company store model employed in the South during the reconstruction era.

Far too many politicians are in the pockets of these big banking institutions, some of them described as "too big to fail." What a load of nonsense. If they are too big to fail, they are too big to exist, and most likely got so bloated through nefarious ways, like redlining and toxic mortgages. We need representative leadership to come into power that says, "Any financial institution, regardless of size that engages in perpetuating systemic racism

63. This is a huge problem for poor districts. See: Mader, "Back to School, but without Books and Basics in Mississippi."

64. For a readable analysis of these patterns of intelligence see: Markova, *The Open Mind.*

65. Mui, "For Black Americans, Financial Damage from Subprime Implosion Is Likely to Last."

by redlining or giving out toxic mortgages will have their assets frozen immediately and the prosecution of those in leadership positions at those institutions will begin forthwith." If banking CEO's and other corporate higher ups were handled like a poor black kid caught with a joint in his pocket, things would change in a hurry. People who have been adversely affected by exploitative lending should immediately have all their debt completely forgiven. Where are the politicians and voters who will stand up for the "least of these" by following the Golden Rule, which Jesus said summed up the entire Torah?

In order to distract people from much of the political manipulation that favors only a small percentage of people, political parties and politicians use wedge issues as another means to divide and conquer an unwitting populace. They pander to single issue voters, which gives them a great deal of leeway on other issues, allowing them tighten their control over others, increase surveillance, concentrate wealth into fewer hands, and profit from warfare among other things. Issues such as a woman's right to choose, gun control, and gay marriage are amongst these issues today. Let me encourage people now to use the Golden Rule and the Ethics of Permaculture, Creation Care, Neighbor Care, and Future Care, as the rubric when voting for politicians who campaign on these issues. Think about whether or not a politician's stance will harm people, deny them agency, or make it harder to live life, support one's family, or maintain safety, life liberty, and the pursuit of happiness. Does the wedge issue adversely, or potentially adversely, affect the people you know or a family member? Does it adversely affect anyone? Who is making the decision, and for whom,[66] and about whom are they making it? For example, I think it is unreasonable for male politicians (most of whom are white)[67] to decide the laws for a nation as diverse as ours. We need diverse voices to fairly represent the interests, rights, and agency of all Americans, not more androcratic, white supremacy. When we have more diversity in representation, wedge issues become less of a focus, and real issues such as dismantling systems of oppression, getting corporate money out of politics, rebuilding infrastructure, and adequately addressing

66. Who benefits? For example, the NRA spends millions lobbying Congress and supporting political campaigns in order to curtail gun legislation. Politicians, gun manufacturers, ammunition companies, and NRA execs reap the benefits. See: Yablon and Spies, "The NRA Has Already Spent More Money on Lobbying."

67. Bump, "The New Congress Is 80 Percent White, 80 Percent Male and 92 Percent Christian."

climate change from a legislative standpoint all become a great deal more important.

What can we do to better follow the Golden Rule in light of all of this information? First, stop falling for wedge issues. Apply the Golden Rule rubric to all of your voting choices and hold lazy, pandering politicians accountable. Secondly, we can begin asking the question, "*cui bono*" which is Latin for "who benefits" and lending support to progressive causes and politics.[68] Asking, "who benefits?" should be a no brainer when considering legislation and policy enactment. For instance, there is a move to make the minimum wage fifteen dollars per hour in the U.S.[69] This is getting a great deal of support from the poor while getting lambasted by many conservatives and wealthy capitalists. In many places in the U.S. fifteen dollars and hour is barely a living wage if there is more than one mouth to feed,[70] yet conservatives are fear mongering saying that it's too high and will kill economic growth.[71] Who would benefit from keeping the minimum wage below starvation level? Companies that are already raking in huge profits like Wal-Mart, who pays notoriously low wages while encouraging their employees to apply for food stamps and Medicaid.[72] Who would benefit from having the minimum wage raised? Only the millions of people who struggle to make ends meet, who wish they could at a minimum live paycheck to paycheck, but often run out of money well before payday or are working multiple jobs simply to scrape by.

According to the Pew Research Center, as of 2017, 30% of America's workers earn minimum wage or slightly more,[73] yet the costs of living goes up all the time. Earning fifteen dollars an hour is only enough to rent a two-bedroom apartment in twenty-one of the fifty states in the U.S. On average,

68. The abolition of slavery was progressive, maintaining slavery was conservative. Universal suffrage was progressive, only white men being eligible to vote was conservative. Universal single payer health care is a progressive idea, for profit medicine is a conservative one. Each of those progressive ideals have made or would make life materially better for millions of people. That's Neighbor Care in a nutshell. That in my mind is following the Golden Rule and loving my neighbor from a political standpoint.

69. Horovitz, "Fast-Food Strikes Widen into Social-Justice Movement."

70. Glasmeir, "A Calculation of the Living Wage."

71. The reverse is actually true, job creation goes up and the economy gets boosted. See: Wolcott, "2014 Job Creation Faster in States that Raised the Minimum Wage." See also: Patton, "The Facts on Increasing the Minimum Wage."

72. O'Connor, "Walmart Workers Cost Taxpayers $6.2 Billion in Public Assistance."

73. DeSilver, "5 Facts about the Minimum Wage."

according to the report, it takes a wage of $20.30/hour to be able to afford a two-bedroom apartment in America.[74] Do we really want to live in a world where we're literally forcing people to live below the poverty line?[75] Would you want to live with a wage of $7.25/hour that would require 112 hours work just to afford a place to live? I've worked for minimum wage and it is incredibly difficult.

Who benefits from the hue and cry for "lower taxes"? Mostly the wealthy who have more loopholes and tax breaks than the poor. Huge multinational companies often get enormous tax breaks in a system of "socialism for the rich and capitalism for the poor." Consider Walmart again, for as the nation's largest retailer they deserve a great deal of scrutiny, who by giving executive bonuses totaling $298 million were able to receive $104 million in tax breaks in 2014.[76] Almost $300 million went to executives while the rank and file associate has to apply for public assistance and cannot afford health care coverage even if working full time. To me, that is disgusting. Walmart is far from the only company in recent years to exploit the tax system to their benefit. There are large companies that have had years recently when they paid no federal taxes at all despite raking in hundreds of millions of dollars in profit because of tax loopholes that are unavailable to small businesses or individuals.[77] This hits the workforce hardest, while politicians and corporations line their coffers. We can do better if we are diligent and stand up for the "least of these" and love our neighbors regardless of who they are.

I believe that from a political standpoint, that to follow the Golden Rule is to begin or continue supporting progressive causes and to be engaged in social justice activism. This is, I realize, for many people, crazy talk. Yet, progressivism has a tendency to lead to expansion of freedom, greater equality, social justice, peaceful policies, and environmental regulation, all of which are vital at a time when time when the biosphere is in peril, war is rampant, and the gap between rich and poor is widening exponentially. Conservative policies have often led to or perpetuated systems of slavery, systemic bigotry, patriarchal policies, and the worship of money

74. Kimura, "How Much Do You Need to Earn to Afford a Modest Apartment?"

75. Republican voters overwhelmingly oppose increasing the minimum wage to $15 according to the Pew Research report, despite the fact that so many vote against their interest in doing so. Conversely, 82% of democratic voters approve of raising it.

76. Clemente, Salas, and Anderson, "Walmart's Executive Bonuses Cost Taxpayers Millions."

77. Krantz, "27 Giant Profitable Companies Paid No Taxes."

as indicated by U.S. history as previously mentioned. Progressive politics tends to break down barriers between people, while conservative policies wants to build walls, create "us versus them" dynamics, and a concentration of wealth in the hands of the few. To me, the choice between two tracks is obvious because one of them is more closely akin to the Golden Rule than the other. In my opinion, people like Cesar Chavez, Dorothy Day, Martin Luther King Jr, Daniel Berrigan, Harriet Tubman, Helen Keller, and Winona LaDuke, among others are far worthier of praise than empire builders, generals, and the wealthy white capitalists whom society currently lauds. We must step out of our comfortable cocoons and actively apply the Golden Rule in order to create a more just, happy, egalitarian world. A simple way of thinking about your time in the voting booth, is to borrow the mantra of the medical profession: Do no harm. If your vote harms the poor, the marginalized, or perpetuates bigotry, that makes your vote wrong from the standpoint of loving our neighbors. If your vote puts profits over people or over the systems that perpetuate life, it's wrong. Sometimes things really are that simple.

6.

War and Peace

CLIMATE CHANGE AND THE likely weather related chaos that it will bring is the single most important issue facing the world today due to its global nature and potentially irrevocable alteration of the biosphere.[1] It is without a doubt caused by human beings[2] because of our insatiable addiction to burning of fossil fuels despite the obvious impact that the continued burning of ancient sunlight,[3] and subsequent addition of unsafe levels of carbon dioxide to the atmosphere, is having on the biosphere as a whole. We in the global West are like a heroin addict shooting up every last vein to get a fix as we extract oil from tar sands and gas from shale, which are energy intensive and highly polluting processes.[4] Couple that with the wanton destruction of old growth forests and vital rainforest ecosystems[5] around the globe, and climate change could well be the downfall of civilization.[6] The second pressing issue facing humanity, that has similar potential to destroy civilization and perhaps the entire human family, is also a man-made problem. That problem is rampant militarism, and the conflicts and wars that spring forth from it. War directly affects so many, and yet its worst overall effects are on the poorest people of the world.

1. Brunner, Butler, and Swoboda, *Introducing Evangelical Ecotheology*, 53.
2. Union of Concerned Scientists, "How Do We Know that Humans Are the Major Cause of Global Warming?"
3. Fossil fuels are largely the result of photosynthesis, in which plants convert sunlight miraculously into their food. See: Hartmann, *The Last Hours of Ancient Sunlight*.
4. Denchak, "The Dirty Fight Over Canadian Tar Sands Oil."
5. Brunner, Butler, and Swoboda, *Introducing Evangelical Ecotheology*, 56–58.
6. Griffin, "Can Civilization Survive the CO2 Crisis?"

The United States long ago became a country that has "grown mad on war" to borrow a phrase from Martin Luther King, Jr's historic speech, "Beyond Vietnam: Time to Break the Silence."[7] For much of its existence America has been at war or in conflict with other people, be they tribal peoples who refused to cede land or give up their traditional ways of life, its own people in a disastrous and deadly Civil War, the people of other nation states, most often who pose no actual threat to America, and since 2001 we have been at war with a nebulous enemy that falls under the blanket term, "terrorists." America's militarism is completely at odds with the teachings of Jesus, yet many Americans are adamant that the U.S. is a "Christian nation."[8] There is, however, no truth to that myth, nor is there any way to reconcile warfare with the Golden Rule or love of neighbor. They are mutually exclusive.

What drives nations to war and gets citizens to support or even demand it? Several things contribute, but for me the roots are greed, fear, and an "us versus them" mentality that dehumanizes our enemies (which is again in stark contrast to Jesus' teachings for us to "love our enemies"). This mentality is fed by propaganda about which, Nazi commander Hermann Goering, at his trial for war crimes at Nuremberg said:

> Of course, the people don't want war. But after all, it's the leaders of the country who determine the policy, and it's always a simple matter to drag the people along whether it's a democracy, a fascist dictatorship, or a parliament, or a communist dictatorship. Voice or no voice, the people can always be brought to the bidding of the leaders. That is easy. All you have to do is tell them they are being attacked, and denounce the pacifists for lack of patriotism, and exposing the country to greater danger." [9]

Out of this propaganda springs the national mythology that ensures the public that America (or any other militaristic state) is benevolent, good, peaceful, and democratic.[10] Conversely, the enemy is evil, prone to vio-

---

7. Tang, "A Society Gone Mad on War." This speech is available to listen to on the internet and should be a part of every American history curriculum in my opinion. See: Eidenmuller, "Martin Luther King, Jr: A Time to Break Silence (Declaration Against the Vietnam War)."

8. Zahnd, *A Farewell to Mars.*

9. Mikkelson, "Hermann Goering: War Games."

10. This is the myth of redemptive violence that Walter Wink treats in his series on the powers. In simplified terms it says that our enemies' violence is evil, but our violence is good.

lence, oppresses its citizenry, intends to harm us, and hates freedom. I recall George W. Bush telling America that as a nation, we would "punish the evil doers" in response to the September 11, attacks on New York and the Pentagon. The U.S. has been termed "The Great Satan" by some who are deemed our enemies and they have a real point.[11] Theologian Rosemary Radford Ruether notes that:

> since 1950 the military state, with its appendages in professional armies and in rapacious business corporations, which produce military equipment as a major part of international trade, have taken over more and more of the wealth of the world. In a vast enclosure of the world commons, much of the land, sea, and even air space of the earth has been expropriated for the militarized corporate economy.
>
> This military state operates out of a polarized, totalitarian worldview of absolute good against absolute evil. "Good" means our invulnerability and total power over other peoples and world resources. "Evil" is anything that challenges this vulnerability and control. [12]

This passage sums up the military agenda of the United States in a nutshell as espoused in the Project For A New American Century document in 2000, which states: "What we require is a military that is strong and ready to meet both present and future challenges; a foreign policy that boldly and purposefully promotes American principles abroad; and national leadership that accepts the United States' global responsibilities."[13] This is the neoconservative doctrine that led the U.S. into an unjust war in Iraq after the September 11, 2001 World Trade Center and Pentagon attacks, and continues to embroil America in other violent conflicts around the world which kill innocent people for the sake of maintaining superpower status[14] and increasing profits for the military-industrial complex.[15]

As just one recent example of American militarism run amok, consider the 300 innocent civilians who were killed during U.S. led airstrikes

11. Fassihi, "The U.S. Is Still Iran's Great Satan."

12. Ruether, Gaia & God, 266–267.

13. Donnelly, "Rebuilding America's Defenses: Strategy, Forces and Resources for a New Century."

14. Zinn and Arnove, A People's History of the United States, 681.

15. The U.S. invasion of Iraq created a huge windfall for U.S. defense contractors. See: Fifield, "Contractors Reap $138B from Iraq War."

in Raqqa, Syria in just a few months' time in 2017.[16] Civilian casualties are always to be expected, even though military commanders and politicians profess otherwise, in the all-out warfare now engaged in by the United States and other hyper-militarized nations.[17] What possible threat does Syria pose to the people within the geographic borders of United States? None whatsoever. The country is, however, strategically located in the highly contentious Middle East, with all of the natural resources that region has, and its leader, Bashar al-Assad, is credibly alleged to be a tyrant committing atrocities against his own people.[18] This latter fact is likely true, but it must be noted that the United States has a long, sordid history of putting tyrants into power or supporting existing dictatorial regimes, provided that doing so enriched American companies, gave the American military a strategic advantage in a particular region, or gave the U.S. privileged access to valuable resources,[19] and therefore any claims of protecting innocent lives from brutal tyrants is hypocrisy at its worst and should be taken with a huge grain of salt. The list of dictators supported by the United States, some of whom they literally placed in power, is a long one. I give a truncated version here for the uninitiated: Saddam Hussein,[20] The Saudi Royal family,[21] Augusto Pinochet,[22] Castillo Armas,[23] Teodoro Obiang Nguema Mbasogo,[24] Pol Pot,[25] and Hamid Karzai[26] to name only a few.

Just as important to the war machine as is the national mythology, is the demonization of any person or group that stands up for peace and questions the motives for war. Richard Nixon is not the only president to harass, belittle, and to disparage the pro-peace movement. Anytime antiwar activists start to clamor for peace, the U.S. government intervenes, often with the F.B.I. as the entity that attempts to infiltrate those groups dating all the

---

16. Nebehay, "U.N. Says 300 Civilians Killed in U.S.-Led Air strikes in Raqqa." For more information on U.S. military atrocities and civilian deaths, the Vietnam War provides ample evidence. See: Madar, "Vietnam: A War on Civilians."

17. Ruether, *Gaia & God*, 267.

18. Goodman and Chomsky, "The Assad Regime is a Moral Disgrace."

19. Calingaert, "Rethinking U.S. Relations with Dictators."

20. Scribol, "20 Brutal Dictators Supported By the U.S," 10.

21. The Week, "5 Dictators the U.S. Still Supports."

22. RT International, "Obama Unapologetic over U.S Support of Pinochet."

23. "Carlos Castillo Armas."

24. The Week, "5 Dictators the U.S. Still Supports."

25. Pilger, "Friends of Pol Pot."

26. McCoy, "America and the Dictators: From Ngo Dinh Diem to Hamid Karzai."

way back to World War I.[27] The military-industrial complex has a vested interest in keeping dissent as quiet as possible. As will be shown, there is a lot of money to be made with warfare, from arms and munitions sales, defense contracts for civilian companies who support the U.S.' military intervention as mercenaries or by engaging in espionage,[28] and advertising sales for media outlets covering the carnage.

A good historian always searches for credible sources when investigating history. In terms of knowing the U.S. military and its "interventions," there were few more credible sources during his lifetime than Smedley Butler. Major General Smedley Butler, USMC, was at the time of his death the most highly decorated Marine in the history of the Marine Corps. When I was in Marine Corps boot camp in 1990 at the Marine Corps Recruit Depot (MCRD) in San Diego we learned about his exploits during the Boxer Rebellion in China. There, he was lauded as a hero for continuing to man his post under extreme duress and heavy enemy fire. What we did not learn is that after he retired from the Corps after a thirty-three-year long career, he decided to truthfully tell America about the reality of warfare and the government's use of the military forces. He wrote the anti-war classic, *War is a Racket,* in which he said:

> War is a racket. It always has been. It is possibly the oldest, easily the most profitable, surely the most vicious. It is the only one international in scope. It is the only one in which the profits are reckoned in dollars and the losses in lives. A racket is best described, I believe, as something that is not what it seems to the majority of the people. Only a small 'inside' group knows what it is about. It is conducted for the benefit of the very few, at the expense of the very many. Out of war a few people make huge fortunes.[29]

Butler described his military career in similar terms. I provide the entire quote because it is key to the imperative to understand that his statements continue to be true to this day and can explain a great deal about the U.S.'

---

27. Eddington, "Why Are FBI Agents Trammeling the Rights of Antiwar Activists?"

28. From 1997–1999, my ex-wife was stationed at Royal Air force Base Menwith Hill Station in North Yorkshire, England. This base was utilized by American military personnel and hundreds of defense contractors, whose job it is to intercept communications from our national enemies as well as others. Such was the security level, that all of this spy activity took place underground. Menwith Hill Station is a highly contentious within in the United Kingdom and little known even within the American military.

29. Butler, "War is a Racket."

use of military force around the world throughout the twentieth and twenty-first centuries:

> I spent 33 years and four months in active military service and during that period I spent most of my time as a high-class muscle man for Big Business, for Wall Street and the bankers. In short, I was a racketeer, a gangster for capitalism. I helped make Mexico and especially Tampico safe for American oil interests in 1914. I helped make Haiti and Cuba a decent place for the National City Bank boys to collect revenues in. I helped in the raping of half a dozen Central American republics for the benefit of Wall Street. I helped purify Nicaragua for the International Banking House of Brown Brothers in 1902–1912. I brought light to the Dominican Republic for the American sugar interests in 1916. I helped make Honduras right for the American fruit companies in 1903. In China in 1927 I helped see to it that Standard Oil went on its way unmolested. Looking back on it, I might have given Al Capone a few hints. The best he could do was to operate his racket in three districts. I operated on three continents.[30]

What does this have to do with the Golden Rule? Quite simply, everything. Our nation's most recent war has been going on for almost twenty years in the Middle East and like Butler's admissions, the wars in Iraq and Afghanistan literally have *nothing* at all to do with maintaining our freedom or protecting us from some shadowy enemy bent on overthrowing the United States. Rather these military misadventures are *all* about profiting from war in terms of corporate profits and resource acquisition,[31] which happens through the destruction of infrastructure as well as natural capital in foreign countries and the slaughter of millions of our neighbors. For example, the C.I.A. led a regime change coup in Guatemala in 1954 that put Castillo Armas in power at the expense of the nascent movement towards democracy led by Guatemalan President Jacobo Arbenz. The official justification for this action was that Guatemala was being infiltrated by Communists who had designs on bringing down America. Castillo Armas was chosen as the new Guatemalan leader because he would bow down to U.S. authority on behalf of United Fruit Company (UFCO) and restore the ludicrously one-sided agreements that all but eliminated UFCO's taxes and kept the wages for poor Guatemalan plantation workers at starvation levels. UFCO made enormous profits because they saved so much money on taxes and wages.

30. Butler, "War is a Racket."
31. Juhasz, "Why the War in Iraq Was Fought for Big Oil."

The Armas coup became the blueprint for C.I.A. and military intervention around the world. Every subsequent military operation in foreign nations has been about making things more favorable for American (and sometimes its European allies) multinational corporations.[32]

The blueprint reads like this, create an enemy out of thin air or with the flimsiest of evidence, foment dissent and civil unrest, engage in a propaganda campaign in the U.S. press and within the target nation, while simultaneously lending material and or military support to the new regime. These actions are always couched in the language of propaganda which is repeated *ad nauseum*, using such phrases as "fighting for freedom," "democracy," "stopping Godless communism" or the vague, open ended, despicable term, "War on Terror." The sad irony is that the United States engages in more state sponsored terrorism than any other nation on Earth.[33] As evidence, consider the aforementioned support and installment of dictators, the fact that America has the largest nuclear arsenal in the world, is the only nation to drop nuclear bombs on an enemy, routinely have used chemical weapons like napalm with horrifying results,[34] uses unmanned drones to terrorize and kill poor people,[35] and far outspends every other nation on "defense" by a huge margin.[36] U.S. forces are scattered far and wide all over the globe and are routinely used for spurious reasons that hurt our global neighbors in multiple ways.

To ensure that this militarism continues unabated, politicians and big businesses collude to make everything they can about patriotism, glorifying the military, through nationalism and flag waving utilizing propaganda techniques. Nationalism has long been rampant in the United States. We cannot even have a sporting event in America without some absurd, over the top display of nationalism, such as a military color guard on the field or jets doing a fly by over the stadium. The National Football League is

32. I wrote my undergraduate history capstone project paper on the coup in Guatemala. One of the best sources I found in my research were bound government documents in the university library. For an instructive book on the subject, see: Schlesinger, Kinzer, and Coatsworth, *Bitter Fruit: The Story of the American Coup in Guatemala*.

33. Chomsky, "The Long, Shameful History of American Terrorism."

34. PBS, "Napalm and The Dow Chemical Company."

35. Friedersdorf, "Every Person Is Afraid of the Drones."

36. Taylor and Karklis, "This Remarkable Chart Shows How U.S. Defense Spending Dwarfs the Rest of the World."

especially enmeshed with this sort of nationalistic display[37] but is not the only sport to do so.

Last season, I attended two major league baseball games, one in New York and one in Philadelphia, both involving the N.Y. Mets. At both games the national anthem was sung, "God Bless America" was sung, and a military veteran was honored on the field with a folded flag and a photo with a player, all to great applause by the crowd. None of this had anything to do with the wonderful game that is baseball. It was all propaganda of the same type used by fascists regimes,[38] and we've been doing it in America for a long time. By insisting that members of the military (or police for that matter) are "heroes," the established powers ensure that the armed forces are tacitly "above reproach" and therefore not to be questioned or criticized. Anyone who dares criticize the military or America in general is often shouted down by those with scant knowledge of how things actually work. This simple method is highly effective propaganda.

Several years ago, I watched an excellent and highly illuminating film entitled *A State of Mind*.[39] The 2004 documentary was shot by a British film crew in North Korea that told the story of the nation's preparations for the Mass Games, an enormous choreographed gymnastics extravaganza that was a celebration of then leader, Kim Jong Il. The spectacle is mind boggling in its scope and the people involved prepare as if their very lives depend upon their individual performances even though there was no guarantee that their "Leader" would even deign to notice the over the top display with more than a brief wave. It also gave insight into the deification of national leaders and the nation state itself as well as into the daily lives of North Koreans living in Pyongyang and in impoverished rural areas of the country. During one scene, shot in a Pyongyang apartment, the people living in the apartment had the TV on, and a cartoon featuring some soldiers was being shown. As the cartoon was translated, it became obvious that it was propaganda disguised as entertainment. Moments after seeing that scene, I realized that though the language was different the message was *exactly* the same as so many things I'd seen on American TV and in movies. In other words, much of what is on American televisions is propaganda. From cartoons I once watched, like *G.I. Joe* and the *Super Friends*, to hit

37. Schottey, "The Flag and the Shield."

38. In 2006, I made a speech in a class at Millersville University and connected every one of Britt's points to American life. See: Britt, "The 14 Characteristics of Fascism."

39. IMDb, "A State of Mind (2004)."

shows like *24*, to countless Hollywood movies, Americans are unwittingly being influenced by steady doses of propaganda.

Media outlets, despite their 24-hour programming, never seem to truly question the obvious lies and obfuscations that are spouted by the President, whomever that may be, or other national and state level politicians, and they blatantly engage in propaganda themselves. Fox News[40] is comically, unashamedly Orwellian[41] in its programming but certainly isn't alone in doing its utmost to promote the pro-war, pro-capitalist, pro-white agenda.[42] Finding reliable news outlets is difficult, though not impossible. NPR is reasonably informative. Democracy Now![43] is definitely worthy of a mention. Their independent news programs often uncover truths other outlets gloss over or fail to cover altogether.

As a nation we make alliances with other countries and often give vast amounts of money to states that engage in human rights abuses and state sponsored terrorism, such as the oil rich African nation of Chad[44] and the strategically important Central Asian country Uzbekistan[45] to name only two such places. Many of America's European allies engage in the same sort of interventionist, militarism that the U.S. does, notably Great Britain and France, and they will continue to do so until Americans and our European neighbors rise up nonviolently[46] in vast numbers and stop participating in the killing of human beings around the world for economic gain. We must also collectively stop electing those who are determined to serve the cause of the war profiteers. Sometimes nations supported by the U.S. or Europe step out of line, or their puppet leaders start to push back at U.S./European dominance, at which point they are suddenly labeled public enemy number one and their crimes against humanity are made public. The media goes into overdrive and the drums begin to be beat for war against nations with no military capability of invading or sending intercontinental ballistic missiles towards major U.S. cities, or any U.S. city.

40. Fox News viewers are the least informed according to a study by Farleigh Dickinson University. See: Rapoza, "Fox News Viewers Uninformed, NPR Listeners Not."

41. Devega, "Peak Propaganda: Fox News Creates an Alternate Reality."

42. Husband, "Ex-White Supremacist Schools Megyn Kelly on Dog Whistles."

43. Democracy Now!, "Democracy Now!"

44. Turse, "Why Is the U.S. Military So Interested in Chad?" See also: Matfess, "U.S. Support for Chad May Destabilize the Sahel."

45. Spetalnick, "U.S. Lifted Uzbekistan's Rights Ranking as Cotton Field Abuses."

46. For examples of how effective nonviolent direct action can be see: Wink, *Engaging the Powers*, 244–251.

Remember Manuel Noriega of Panama? He was once a friend of George H.W. Bush and was even on the C.I.A.'s payroll[47] despite being known to traffic in cocaine and for being a brutal dictator. Noriega learned some of his dictatorial skills through the U.S.' School of the Americas,[48] a military training school responsible for training some of Latin America's worst human rights abusers, many of whom were supported by the U.S. regardless of which political party was in the White House. By 1989, Noriega became an enemy of America for refusing to cooperate on issues relating to the operation and use of the Panama Canal and for ostensibly killing Americans.[49] As a result, the U.S. launched 'Operation Just Cause' and invaded Panama causing the deaths of hundreds of Panamanian civilians and 24 U.S. armed forces personnel while wounding thousands more innocent Panamanians. Exact numbers of civilian casualties are hard to come by because of cover ups and covert operations tactics. The official reasons given for the invasion were to arrest Noriega, restore democracy to Panama, to protect the canal (a hugely valuable economic asset) and to protect American lives.[50] Instead of democracy, however, a new puppet government was installed and drug trafficking and drug use in Panama increased. That sounds a great deal like the situation in Afghanistan since the 2003 American invasion.

We have a volunteer military in America now. That may change in the future if the draft is reinstated as some have argued be done.[51] All too often those targeted for recruitment into the armed forces come from poor rural areas or inner cities. Like me when I was a Marine, all are unwitting agents of what can only be rationally described as an evil empire based upon the evidence so readily available, some of which has been treated in this chapter. The poor abroad too are the most affected by war and economic sanctions, as can be seen in Palestine, for example, where basic human rights and the ability to meet basic human needs are denied to those who are Palestinian by the terroristic actions of the Israeli government and by extension, the United States,[52] whose hundreds of millions of dollars

47. Ghosh, "Who's Who on the CIA Payroll."

48. SOA Watch, "Notorious Graduate." This training school at Ft. Benning Georgia has since been renamed the Western Hemisphere Institute for Security and Cooperation. See: The United States Army, "WHINSEC."

49. Walters, "Just Cause and Its Aftermath." See also: Grandin, "How America's 1989 Invasion of Panama Explains the Current U.S. Foreign Policy Mess."

50. Zinn and Arnove, *A People's History*, 593–594.

51. Korb and Goepel, "The Case for the Draft."

52. Greenwald, "U.S. Admits Israel Is Building Permanent Apartheid Regime."

support Israeli apartheid policies.[53] America's rhetoric, that we as a nation are bringing freedom and helping the oppressed is shown to be fallacious by its actual actions or its inaction.[54] For example, the U.S. stood by and did nothing as Hitler slaughtered countless Jews in the late 1930s and early 1940s,[55] when South Africa was ruled by apartheid laws,[56] or when there was genocide taking place in Rwanda[57] to name just three such examples of American inaction in the face of actual tyranny.

It is only where there is some resource to gain control over, be it strategic or profitable, that America's military is deployed. This explains why I was awoken as an 18-year-old less than two weeks prior to leaving for the MCRD in San Diego, CA by a phone call from my cousin Eric. Without any words of greeting or context, he said into the phone, "Saddam Hussein invaded Kuwait. You're going to war." It was August 2, 1990, I was hungover from a night of juvenile, pre-boot camp drunkenness and I lieterally had no idea who Saddam Hussein was, nor did I have any idea of the precise location where Kuwait could be found on a map. Fortunately, even though I did get screamed at repeatedly by my drill instructors that I would soon die in a desert war zone, I did not in fact end up in the Persian Gulf for Operation Desert Storm, by the grace of God. I was merely a minor cog in the war machine of a war that was primarily about one thing: Oil. [58]

Without a regimented, systematic overhaul of human behavior, most people would not consider hurting or killing another human being. The armed forces use boot camps to achieve just such a change. When Smedley Butler said that most military personnel don't have any thoughts of their own, he was right. The process of military training attempts to turn soldiers, sailors, Marines, and airmen into mindless drones who will follow orders instantly without analysis or critical thinking. Instructors also demonize the enemy to make them "less than human." For the Marines, the process begins at once, while still at the airport.

53. Eglash, "Is Israel an 'Apartheid' State?" See also: Rabinovitch, Nichols, and Perry, "Israel Imposes Apartheid Regime on Palestinians."

54. Zinn and Arnove, *A People's History*, 408.

55. Zinn and Arnove, *A People's History*, 409.

56. Zinn and Arnove, *A People's History*, 568. See also: Elizabeth Kolbert, "Tutu, in New York, Calls for Economic Sanctions."

57. Zinn and Arnove, *A People's History*, 655.

58. Ahmed, "Iraq Invasion Was about Oil."

Uniformed drill instructors began that process when I arrived in San Diego by arbitrarily assigning recruits to a platoon and then putting us on a bus to the recruit depot. There, after an intentionally bewildering drive from the nearby airport, another drill instructor began to scream at the now nervous group of American youths to "Get on my yellow footprints! NOW!" From there the indoctrination began with a profoundly exhausting first week, where recruits were purposefully deprived of sleep and herded like sheep to do administrative tasks, get haircuts and get our uniforms and hygiene gear issued, all while having a generally befuddled sense of "what have I gotten myself into?" We were taught early on during our thirteen weeks of boot camp that our new priorities were to be "God, country, and Corps" even before our families and that our individuality was a thing of the past. We learned the skills that were necessary to "locate, close with, and *destroy* my enemy"[59] by any means necessary[60] and to shout mantras like, "Kill the ragheads, bury 'em in the sand."[61] This is how trained killers are made and is how we learn to see the other human beings as "enemies" rather than as people. Turning people into trained killers is not the way to love our neighbor or do unto others. For me, learning these things are the biggest sins of my life.

Politicians play their part in this satanic ritual of death and destruction through the use of wedge issues that divide and conquer the voting public. By having us focus so much energy and attention on things like abortion, gun control, or LGBTQIA rights, though all of them are important, they distract us from even bigger issues, such as systemic racism and rampant militaristic war mongering. Consider the numbers for the U.S. defense budget (a misnomer if there ever was one) for the 2017 fiscal year. According to the Department of Defense's (DoD) website, the 2017 discretionary spending for the military and related "defense" agencies is

59. Simmons, "Locate, Close with and Destroy."

60. During our many hours of hand to hand combat training we were told to be as vicious as was could be in those situations and if possible we were to peel the side of the enemies face off with our combat boots when stomping on said enemies face. During this move we would shout, "SWEEP AND STOMP!"

61. This mantra was shouted out by the recruits of Echo Company, platoon 2074, led by Senior Drill Instructor Staff Sergeant Tyrone Keniry, when they climbed the thirty-foot rope on the obstacle course. Keniry would have been my Senior D.I. had I not gone on the buddy program with a friend from high school. We were separated at the airport by the aforementioned Marine who arbitrarily put the new recruits into platoons. The first day of training I was given the choice to stay with SSgt. Keniry or to move downstairs to Platoon 2073 to "go be with my little friend" as Keniry so eloquently put it.

$582,000,000,000.[62] The DoD claims that this exorbitant amount of money is needed because "The budget request reflects the priorities necessary for our force today and in the future to best serve and protect our nation in a rapidly changing security environment."[63] This is laughable when considering the historical evidence that the continental U.S. has not been invaded by a foreign power since 1812[64] and an invasion is incredibly unlikely given the size of America's stockpile of intercontinental weapons of mass destruction. The American military, however, has invaded, encroached, bombed, and "occupied" countries all over the globe that were no threat to the U.S. at all, with the exception of "American capital" or "American interests." American diplomats for example proclaimed that something needed to be done to protect American capital and called on the government to intervene because of the democratic reforms taking place in Guatemala in the late 1940s until the mid-50s.[65] That type of call to action began in 1893 when Sanford B. Dole requested that the U.S. Marines land in Hawai'i[66] so his businesses could make even more money than they already were, and it continues to do so to this day.[67]

That $582 billion supports a force of 1,214,500 soldiers in the Army, including active, reserve and civilian support, 564,200 naval personnel, 662,000 Air Force personnel, and 245,000 Marine Corps personnel.[68] Also included in the military arsenal of the United States are: ninety-six operational bombers, 450 intercontinental ballistic missiles (nuclear weapons), forty-nine tactical fighter squadrons, 304 naval ships, and fifty-four army brigade combat teams.[69] Those numbers are simply staggering. It is worth noting that every single empire in recorded history that overspent on mili-

62. U.S. Department of Defense. "Department of Defense (DoD) Releases Fiscal Year 2017."

63. U.S. Department of Defense. "Department of Defense (DoD) Releases Fiscal Year 2017."

64. Dotinga, "Why America Forgets the War of 1812." The September 11 attacks were carried out by an organization rather than a foreign power. See also: Noam Chomskey, "Not Since the War of 1812."

65. Schlesinger, Kinzer, and Coatsworth, *Bitter Fruit*.

66. The History Channel, "Americans Overthrow Hawaiian Monarchy."

67. The pineapple fields around Wahiawa, Hawai'i on the island of Oahu continue to grow monocrops of pineapples. The Dole Plantation has also gotten into the tourism trade. See: Dole Plantation, "Dole Plantation: Hawaii's Complete Pineapple Experience."

68. Pike, "U.S. Military Personnel End Strength."

69. Department of Defense, "Fiscal Year 2017 Budget Request."

tary personnel, equipment, and operations has crumbled.[70] It is also worth noting again that war is a racket, a for profit enterprise, and that every single one of the 2.118 million men and women of the armed forces are being used to profit upon the deaths, dismemberment, disenfranchisement, ecological destruction, and neocolonial subjugation of people around the world through "regime changes" and the "War on Terror." Imagine the tremendous good that could be done with $582 billion and remember that number the next time a politician claims that there is no money for universal health care, veterans' services, food stamps, social security, or education benefits. Eisenhower was right to warn us of the "military-industrial complex."

Unfortunately, his warning went unheeded despite his intimate knowledge of the American war machine. President Trump has asked for further increases in the nuclear arsenal in order to start a new arms race,[71] and even bemoaned the fact that he couldn't just use the nukes, according to conservative pundit Joe Scarborough.[72] Lest we forget, the Cold War was a frightening time fraught with threats, counter threats, proxy wars, and films like *The Day After,* which dramatized a fictional nuclear attack on Kansas.[73] We did "duck and cover" drills at school when I lived in Kansas City, MO in the early 1980s, and air raid sirens that went off during other drills. The current president seemingly wants us to go through all of that again.

Asking, "who benefits?" in relation to matters of war and peace is simply common sense. Who would benefit from a war in Iraq? Defense contractors, fossil fuel companies, media conglomerates with ratings and advertising dollars to think about, government agency employees whose livelihoods are tied to foreign policy issues, glory hunting military leaders wanting to create a name for themselves, and politicians who want power and monetary kickbacks. Because I researched the government documents related to the Guatemalan coup in 1954 and cross referenced them with contemporary news accounts about Guatemala and the democratic developments happening there,[74] I am now incredibly skeptical any time

70. See: Kennedy, *The Rise and Fall of the Great Empires.*

71. Mosher, "Trump Wants to Make Nuclear Weapons Easier to Use."

72. Belvedere, "Trump Reportedly Asks Why U.S. Can't Use Nukes."

73. IMDb, "The Day After (TV Movie 1983)."

74. The lies and obfuscations during that time were published in newspapers around the country and painted a red herring to convince the American public that Soviet Russia was taking over the Guatemalan government to put a communist regime within striking distance of the U.S.

I read or hear about a "rogue government" that needs to be replaced in some resource rich or strategically located country. All too often the propagandists demonize democratic reformers, praise dictators favorable to U.S. investors, and conveniently forget to mention when violently oppressive regimes are in fact supported, if not wholly propped up, by U.S. money and arms. For these reasons, I always want to know "who benefits?" Knowing who benefits can inform me in how to apply the Golden Rule and the ethics of permaculture in a given situation.

It is equally important to know who is directly affected by war. Who are the victims of carpet bombing campaigns, small arms fire, occupying forces, propaganda, brutal regimes, destruction and the disruption of every aspect of normal, daily life? It is the common person on the street, the poor, the systemically oppressed, and those facing dead end futures. Let us first look at the members of the armed forces in the U.S. Many of the people who joined the military did it for reasons other than patriotic zeal, which does occasionally happen, with former NFL star Pat Tillman being a high-profile example, though his attitude changed when he realized the war in Iraq was not about freedom or democracy.[75]

As a seventeen-year-old in rural North Texas, I wanted nothing more than to "get out of Dodge" in order to escape a physically abusive, emotionally neglected upbringing and an uncertain future. At the time of my enlistment, I had no real plans for college because I had no way to pay for it other than a small drama scholarship to a local junior college, and I also had a desire to travel in order to be as far away from Texas as I could get. One morning in 1989, before one of our basketball games, a friend and teammate of mine's father was extolling the virtues of the Marine Corps reserve, which his son had just signed up for, and I was all ears. Joining the Marines, I was told, would give me a chance to travel and a way to pay for college,[76] and might even allow me to play basketball with the All-Marine team. I would also have a paycheck, medical and dental benefits, and would qualify for thirty days paid vacation per year. Talk about incentive. Where else could I land a job with benefits like that as an 18-year-old with little job experience other than farm work? I decided to join as an active duty Marine for four years rather than as a reservist for six. The Navy, after seeing my test scores, had offered me training on a nuclear submarine in return for

75. Devereaux, "The NFL, the Military, and the Hijacking of Pat Tillman's Story."

76. The G.I. Bill I received for my active duty tour from 1990–1994 was woefully insufficient to pay for a four year college degree.

an eight-year commitment. I politely declined and joined the Marines. The military offered me and countless others a way out. Most of the guys I was in boot camp with were between the ages of eighteen and twenty. The oldest recruit was twenty-six. We were all young and were sold by the promises of our recruiters, who are a great deal like used car sales people, only they wear a spiffy uniform. Many of us were poor, either from inner cities or rural areas like Blue Ridge, Texas where I had grown up between the ages of eleven and eighteen. Boot camp, in many ways, was thirteen weeks of toxic stress, sleep deprivation, training to kill, and indoctrination.

Young men and women, many of whom are too young to buy a beer in a bar in most places in America, are recruited, trained and readied for war. During times of economic recession when sixteen to twenty-four year olds have a hard time finding jobs, recruiters have an easier time of getting young adults to sign on the dotted line.[77] In 2013, 44% of new military recruits came from the South, despite the fact that the South only has 36% of the eighteen to twenty-four year old population nationwide.[78] Unsurprisingly, the poorest states in the United States are in the South.[79] Minority recruitment has increased from 25% to 40% between 1990 and 2015,[80] which is not surprising given that the wealth of black and Latino families is declining in America.[81] Sociological research from 2008 bears out these numbers and remains valid. Amy Lutz, a sociologist at Syracuse University, found that those who come from families with lower incomes join the military more readily than those from more affluent families.[82] As in my case, the incentives are high for a kid who cannot afford to go to college or a trade school. How many Americans would love to have universal healthcare, for instance, which is given to military members and their families. A career in the military seems like a great option but comes at a huge price even if those who join do not die in a war zone. Live or die, they contribute to the deaths of their global neighbors at the hands of the U.S. military who are often poor themselves.

77. Department of Defense, "Population Representation in the Military Services 2014."

78. Bender, Kiersz, and Rosen, "Some States Have Much Higher Enlistment Rates than Others."

79. Dillinger, "U.S. Poverty Level by State."

80. Parker, Cilluffo, and Stepler, "6 Facts about the U.S. Military and Its Changing Demographics."

81. Hoxie, "Blacks and Latinos Will Be Broke in a Few Decades."

82. Lutz, "Who Joins the Military?"

Thus it has always been. The rich and powerful find reasons to go to war and then get the poor to do the fighting, killing, and dying for them. History is replete with atrocities, lives cut too short, whole villages, towns, or even cities razed to the ground. For well over a century now, the United States has been at the forefront of military campaigns to secure resources, maintain personnel in strategic locations, and in selling arms to allies who do the Pentagon's bidding. Millions upon millions have died as a result of U.S. military interventions.[83] Recently, former President Barack Obama tweeted a positive response to the Parkland High School students who have been standing up to the National Rifle Association after their school was terrorized by a young man with multiple mental health issues, killing seventeen people.[84] In the tweet, he wrote: "Young people have lead all of our great movements. How inspiring to see it again, in so many smart, fearless students standing up for their rights to be safe; marching and organizing to remake our world as it should be. We've been waiting for you. And we've got your backs."[85] When I read these words, my first thought was, "What about all of the children in Pakistan, Yemen, Afghanistan, and Iraq? Do they not deserve the same right to be safe from U.S. bombs and bullets?" This type of hypocrisy, that says only American lives are worthy, is clearly not what the wise sages of every faith had in mind when they came up with their versions of the Golden Rule. Jesus of Nazareth, certainly did not think that killing of any kind was ever warranted,[86] even when he was being beaten, mocked, and crucified. Nor was elevating one group above another. He showed this by speaking to the Samaritan woman at the well, healing a Roman centurion's daughter despite the fact that the Romans were an occupying, tyrannical force in Palestine, and spending time with publicans (the tax collectors who were the bane of the existence of many Jews during Jesus' lifetime.)

Violence begets more violence as history has shown and various spiritual traditions proclaim.[87] Judaism and Christianity's scriptural traditions speak of this in multiple accounts, including the Cain and Abel story

---

83. Tirman, "Why Do We Ignore the Civilians Killed in American Wars?" See also: Grossman, "From Wounded Knee to Syria."

84. Ovalle and Blaskey, "Parkland School Shooter Nikolas Cruz Makes First Live Appearance in Court."

85. Brinlee, "Obama Tweets to Parkland Students."

86. Zahnd, *Farewell to Mars*, 96.

87. The Buddha, "The Dhammapada."

which leads to the Biblical flood because people had become so violent.[88] A militant Palestinian, pushed to his wits ends by the oppression of Israel's apartheid policies, denial of human rights and access to the basic necessities of life, fires a rocket into Israel, and then Israel responds with an exponential increase in violence with missiles into Palestine[89] thus creating more hatred, more death, and more violence. Both acts of violence are wrong according to the teachings of Jesus and both only serve to create more violence.

We must be far more proactive in our demands to create a more peaceful world by holding our politicians accountable. As citizens we have the power and the right to ensure that our tax dollars are supporting programs and actions which are life giving, Earth restoring, peace promoting, as well as engaging in restorative justice, diplomacy, and reparations for the wrongs we have done. Those whom our government scapegoats and calls terrorists do not hate America because we as a nation are a bastion of freedom and democracy. Rather they hate America for the approximately 130 years of U.S. imperialism around the globe, our staunch support of Israel, actions like overthrowing the Iranian government after it nationalized its oil industry,[90] and the invasion and occupation of Iraq. Interviews with captured ISIS fighters have revealed that the organization often recruits people whose lives have been damaged by the American occupation in Iraq.

Imagine if some foreign power took over your hometown, started dropping bunker busting bombs indiscriminately, or flew unmanned drones that dropped bombs on the homes of people you know. How would you feel? Imagine a whole city being leveled by untold tons of ordnance and napalm like the bombing campaigns of the Korean War that killed off 20% of the North Korean population according to one U.S. general.[91] Do you think you and your family would forget such atrocities? Imagine being a Syrian citizen who just wants peace but is caught in up in a geopolitical power game where superpowers vie for control of the country in a proxy war, as bombs fall from the sky blasting ancient cities to rubble while leaving ordinary people cowering in basements petrified with fear.[92] Most don't care if the bombs are coming from Assad's regime and his Russian allies, or

88. Zahnd, *A Farewell to Mars*, 59–60.

89. Arenheim, "Israel Strikes 40 Hamas Targets."

90. Zinn and Arnove, *People's History*, 438–439.

91. Harden, "The U.S. War Crime North Korea Won't Forget."

92. van Tets, "Exodus: Terrified Syrians Dash to Flee Air Strikes."

if they come from the U.S. and its allies. They just want them to stop. We are complicit in these acts when we do not *demand* that America's military stand down. We are complicit when we continue to laud the military as heroes, wave our flags, and engage in excessive nationalism because doing so insulates us from the horrific and evil nature of war.[93]

American pacifist A.J. Muste said, "There is no way to peace; peace is the way."[94] Warfare is unsustainable and ecologically damaging to the planet and robs human beings of life. We cannot love our neighbors with violence or by turning a blind eye to our national violence while we sit comfortably in our homes watching TV, surfing the Internet, or engaging in any other activity in safety far from the falling bombs and the whizzing of bullets. We cannot love our neighbors when we sit in silence when we learn that a local teen has enlisted into the U.S. military. We can love our neighbors by standing up for and demanding peace, by telling the truth about matters of war (as I have attempted to do here), and by educating our children in the ways of peacemaking.

We can love our neighbors by righting the wrongs of our warmongering past with our time, talent, and money. We can love our neighbors by seeing every human being as worthy of life, liberty, and the pursuit of happiness. We can love our neighbors and do unto them as we would have them do unto us by refusing to scapegoat them, refusing to retaliate, refusing to participate in warmongering, and laying down our weapons. A failure to do so will have dire consequences for our neighbors in far flung countries and for us as well, for we are all in this together, and the violence won't stop until we make it do so.

93. Astore, "Why It's Wrong to Equate Military Service with Heroism."
94. Ward, "There Is No Way to Peace, Peace Is the Way."

7.

Permaculture
A Brief Introduction

IN THE BIBLICAL STORY of creation, humankind, both male and female, are created in the image of God and placed in the Garden of Eden, and we've been trying to get back there ever since.[1] In many ways, permaculturists work to design cultivated ecosystems that would resemble that mythical place, where we read that Eden was profoundly abundant in providing all of the needs of those first two people with comparatively little effort on their part, in a place of unsurpassed natural beauty. A common permaculture joke is that people who practice permaculture are lazy and constantly ask, "What less can I do?" Behind this joke lies the notion that a highly effective permaculture design will design as much of the repetitive and arduous work out of the system as possible so that people have more time to enjoy their own personal gardens of Eden, like Adam and Eve did before the wily serpent enters the story, as well as spending more time with family, friends, and community. During my Advanced Permaculture Design Course (APDC) in Permaculture Teaching in 2010, permaculture teacher and designer Jude Hobbs[2] quipped that permaculture is a revolution disguised as organic gardening. Indeed, she is correct, as will be seen in this chapter, and so were those wise sages who each came up with their culturally expressed Golden Rule, as was shown in the previous chapters.

1. Dave Jacke explores the theme of recreating an Edenic paradise in chapter 2 of volume one. See: Jacke and Toensmeier, *Edible Forest Gardens*, vol. 1, 25–53.

2. For more on Hobbe's design and teaching, see: Cascadia Permaculture, "Jude Hobbs: Permaculture Design Courses and Teacher Trainings."

In this chapter, the reader will be given a necessarily brief introduction to permaculture design,[3] its ethics and principles, examples of its efficacy, as well as the reasons it is so badly needed.

Bill Mollison, the Tasmanian-born logger turned biologist and academic, defined permaculture in *Permaculture: A Designer's Manual* (commonly referred to as "The Designer's Manual") thus:

> Permaculture (permanent agriculture) is the conscious design and maintenance of agriculturally productive ecosystems which have the diversity, stability, and resilience of natural ecosystems. It is the harmonious integration of landscape and people, providing their food, energy, shelter, and other material and non-material needs in a sustainable way. Without permanent agriculture there is no possibility of a stable social order. Permaculture design is a system of assembling conceptual, material, and strategic components in a pattern which functions to benefit life in all its forms.[4]

That sounds like a description of Eden to me and a well-designed piece of land looks like it too. Permaculture as permanent agriculture is merely a good first step. As ecological designer and author Dave Jacke told me in an interview a recently, we need to move towards culture design, to design cultures from an anthropological sense, and doing effective permaculture design for food, fuel, and fiber is the foundation of that culture. Jacke noted that permaculture currently uses resources, tools, and technology well in terms of landscapes and forest gardens, but that we need to improve our design of social and economic structures as well as work on our own inner landscapes (what I call Zone 0, of which more will be said later) so that interpersonal and societal dysfunction do not disrupt the system.[5] For our purposes here, we will treat permaculture as a landscape design system for the sake of brevity. All of the following principles can and are, however, applied to designing social systems, businesses, educational endeavors, and more.

Permaculture is a form of systems thinking. Donella Meadows defined a system in this way: "A system is a set of things – people, cells, molecules, or whatever – interconnected in such a way that they produce their own

---

3. Two of the design related books I have are over 550 pages apiece and there are now dozens of books on permaculture and hundreds more on various techniques used in permaculture designs.

4. Mollison, *Permaculture: A Designer's Manual*, ix.

5. Jacke, "Dave Jacke Interview," telephone interview by author, March 19, 2018.

pattern of behavior over time."[6] Permaculturists seek to design systems that create a variety of different yields that are not only sustainable, but also regenerative. "An important function of almost every system is to ensure its own perpetuation,"[7] which fits with the idea of a well-designed, cultivated ecosystem, which is patterned after naturally occurring, healthy ecosystems. Through the intentional design process, the designer works within the limits of the design site to enhance certain positive elements, for instance, a south facing growing area that creates a microclimate[8] that can extend the growing season by taking advantage of the sun's rays even during the winter, while mitigating potentially negative elements, such as high winds that could potentially damage crops or buildings. The resilience of a site is of paramount importance, particularly in light of global climate change. "Ecological disasters in many places come from loss of resilience, as species are removed from ecosystems, soil chemistry and biology are disturbed, or toxins build up."[9] A good design will bring diverse elements together that work harmoniously with one another, hopefully with each element symbiotically working with multiple other elements, to foster diversity not for diversity's sake, but for a more resilient system of "beneficial functional connections."[10]

The ethical underpinnings of permaculture are expressed in a variety of ways. My own way of espousing them is theological – Creation Care, Neighbor Care, and Future Care. Mollison, having studied community ethics that had been adopted by religious and cooperative groups, synthesized his findings into three ethical principles. "1) Care for the Earth: Provision for all life systems to continue and multiply. 2) Care of People: Provision for people to access those resources necessary to their existence. 3) Setting Limits to Population and Consumption: By governing our own needs, we can set aside resources to further the above principles."[11] He also names a prime directive of permaculture, which is to make the ethical decision "to

6. Meadows, *Thinking in Systems*, 2.

7. Meadows, *Thinking in Systems*, 15.

8. A microclimate is a small area where temperature, moisture level, or wind velocity is markedly different from the surrounding area. Identifying these areas on a site allows designers to create niches for increased yields.

9. Meadows, *Thinking in Systems*, 78.

10. Mollison, *Permaculture*, 32.

11. Mollison, *Permaculture*, 2.

take responsibility for our own existence and that of our children."[12] When we shift focus from thinking in terms of "what can I get from" a landscape or another person, to, "What does this person, or land, have to give if I cooperate with them?" we move towards an ethical way of being, that can lead to peace and plenty for all concerned.[13] This is the essence of loving our neighbors and enacting the Golden Rule, for other people, as well as the flora and fauna that we all benefit from and rely on for survival.

David Holmgren, the co-originator of permaculture with Mollison, says that the Care of the Earth begins with care for the soil, which when healthy teems with life, because "profligate use of the soil can result in a rapid loss of its capacity to support life."[14] As we saw in Chapter Two, the current industrialized agriculture model is woefully detrimental to soil health due to repetitive plowing, erosion and soil loss, and chemical applications that destroy the biota of the soil. We need an agricultural ethic and praxis that regenerates the soil, leaving it better and more fertile for future generations of land stewards. We must also in our care for the earth do all we can to foster and maintain biological diversity, even when those life forms are inconvenient to us.[15] Animals have their roles to play in ecosystems just as humans do, and some are incredibly important. Consider the prairie dog. These adorable, burrowing mammals are known as a keystone species,[16] which is a species that is "critical for the survival of other species in its community."[17] In other words, without prairie dogs, the entire grassland ecosystems that they live in would collapse. Despite their keystone role, prairie dogs are being decimated by human beings who find them to be a nuisance. They do not realize the harm that they are inflicting on America's prairies and the life that once thrived there. We need to cooperate with nature rather than attempt to dominate it, for, "cooperation, not competition, is the very basis of future survival and of existing life systems."[18]

Caring for people is the essence of both the Golden Rule and loving our neighbors, as well as an ethic of permaculture design. Because human beings have the mental acuity and the physical ability to affect our

12. Mollison, *Permaculture*, 1.

13. Mollison, *Permaculture*, 3.

14. Holmgren, *Principles and Pathways*, 5.

15. Holmgren, *Principles and Pathways*, 6.

16. Defenders of Wildlife, "Basic Facts About Prairie Dogs."

17. Johns, "Keying in on Keystone Species."

18. Mollison, *Permaculture*, 34.

environments, permaculture's second ethic is an anthropocentric environmental philosophy "which places human needs and aspirations as our central concern" through focusing on "accepting responsibility for our situation as much as possible," as well as focusing on "opportunities rather than obstacles" as we care for ourselves, our neighbors, and future generations.[19] As Holmgren notes, this anthropocentric idea to "look after yourself first," is not an invitation to abject selfishness and avarice; rather it is, "a challenge to grow up through self – reliance and personal responsibility."[20] We can implement this by thinking deeply about many of the issues raised in this book, as well as others not treated herein, and by applying our learning mindfully in ways that will affect not just ourselves, but our neighbors next door, those downstream, and others all around the world. It means that those of us in wealthy nations like the U.S. need to voluntarily limit our consumption and reproduction, and advocate for the reallocation of resources. Holmgren writes:

> Setting Limits to Consumption and Reproduction requires us to consider what is enough, and sometimes to make hard decisions. When we accept our own mortality and limited power, the setting of our own personal limits becomes a reasonable bargain with the world. We maintain our autonomy and self-control by exercising self-restraint, and so reduce the likelihood that some external force or power will force us to change. . . . In thinking about what is enough, we have to look at the needs and wants that drive material gain, and also the capacity of earth and people to provide those needs and wants. The ecological footprint is one simple method to audit and reorganise our personal demand for natural resources. Such methods help us set limits and monitor our performance.[21]

Americans live unsustainably and setting limits to consumption has not been something we have societally done well. In fact, during the presidency of George W. Bush, Ari Fleischer suggested that America's per capita energy consumption was "the American way of life" and that there would be no push to correct the imbalance of Americans using more energy per capita than any other country on earth.[22] It is time, in the name of Neighbor Care, to seriously apply the third ethic of permaculture as espoused by Mollison

19. Holmgren, *Principles and Pathways*, 6–7.

20. Holmgren, *Principles and Pathways*, 7.

21. Holmgren, *Principles and Pathways*, 8–9.

22. The White House, "Press Briefing by Ari Fleischer."

and Holmgren (and differently by my ethical third term, Future Care). The planet is currently beyond its carrying capacity, meaning we are using up resources unsustainably and producing more waste than the planet can handle. It would take 1.7 Earths to sustain this level of production and waste,[23] which is problematic given that we only have one Earth to live on. The ecological footprint is determined by measuring the global hectares available (GHA), the unit of measure that encompasses the productive capacity of the planet's arable land, seas, and forests in a given year.[24] As of 2013, the latest available data, the U.S. would need 8.6 GHA to sustain current levels of consumption which overshoots the available GHA by 4.8 GHA.[25] Measured in acres, the numbers seem even more stark. There are approximately 4.5 acres per person on earth available to meet an individual's needs. Americans, however, are living off about 24 acres per person while the global average is 5.6/person.[26] We, particularly as Americans, are robbing from our neighbors with this level of rapacious consumption and doing great harm to the biosphere as well. Applying permaculture and related systems of ecological design, as a concrete way of loving our neighbors and doing to them as we would have done to us, is clearly needed if we are not to become "the final plague."[27]

Like the ethics, the principles of permaculture are espoused in different ways. For our purposes here, I will rely on the work of Mollison first, and then Holmgren. There will be some overlap, but Holmgren's principles are more in depth and deserve a full treatment of all twelve as he outlines them. That said, Mollison's are instructive, and I will begin with these "Mollisonisms" as they are sometimes called. There are five Mollisonian permaculture principles found in 'The Designer's Manual'. The first of these is to work with nature instead of working against it in order to facilitate nature's development. Too often we work against nature and then wonder why we have to keep adding poisons to a landscape, or do unnecessary repetitive work, like we do in our yards. There are no monocrops found in nature, but the entire lawn care industry is predicated upon maintaining a monocropped lawn of uniform grass at enormous cost in terms of energy, pollution, and make-work. The second of Mollison's principles is,

23. Global Footprint Network, "Ecological Footprint."
24. Bower, "Comparing the Ecological Footprints of America and the E.U."
25. Global Footprint Network, "Ecological Wealth of Nations."
26. Merkel, "Global Living Project."
27. Mollison, *Permaculture*, 7.

"the problem is the solution; everything works both ways."[28] By changing our mindsets, as Holmgren's quote above noted, we can see solutions more readily. Mollison was fond of saying that having too many slugs in a garden was not the problem; rather the problem was not having introduced ducks to the garden to feed on the readily available slugs. In this view a slug is a resource!

His third principle is "make the least change for greatest effect" (more will be said on this below). From a theoretical standpoint, the yield of a system is limited only by the imagination of the designer and the information they have available to them, is Mollison's fourth principle. By being imaginative, playful, and thinking outside the box, we can conceivably find more ways to use a resource to get more sustainable yields.[29] Last, Mollison believed that "everything gardens, or has an effect on its environment.[30] Think of a chicken scratching around in the grass looking for food, burrowing animals shifting soil around, or elephants knocking over trees to get forage as a way to understand this last Mollisonism.

To work with nature instead of against it we need to use our resources wisely. To enable us to do so, Mollison classified resources[31] as: 1) "Those that increase with modest use" such as green browse (the plants, shrubs, and trees that certain animals such as deer or goats selectively eat) or information which can flourish when exchanged freely. 2) "Those unaffected by use," such as favorable climate conditions, a nice view, a pile of large rocks that collects heat or prevents erosion, and well managed ecosystems. 3) "Those which disappear or degrade if not used" such as unharvested fruit, unused annual and perennial crops, insect swarms (bees and grasshoppers[32]) irruptions of fish, and water run-off during heavy rains.[33]

28. Mollison, *Permaculture*, 35.

29. Mollison, *Permaculture*, 35.

30. Mollison, *Permaculture*, 17, 35.

31. Mollison, *Permaculture*, 16, 35.

32. Grasshoppers are a nutrient dense food source. I have eaten them cooked in Oaxaca, Mexico, and raw during a rewilding class that focused on primitive skills such as trapping, fashioning cordage from plant fibers, fire making, and finding different food sources like insects and forage plants. Eating insects is common throughout the world and insects are an underutilized resource in America. See: Guynup and Ruggia, "For Most People, Eating Bugs Is Only Natural."

33. Water run-off is a huge problem for many areas, such as Lancaster, Pennsylvania where rainwater overwhelms the combined sewer system leading to raw sewage being discharged into the watershed of Lancaster County. See: United States Environmental Protection Agency, "The City of Lancaster, PA Clean Water Act Settlement."

4) "Those reduced by use" such as forests, fish and game stocks, mineral deposits, and nonrenewable resources like coal, uranium, oil, and phosphorus. 5) "Those which pollute or destroy if used" such as toxic poisons introduced into ecosystems, radioactive substances, super-highways, islands of concrete in cities and suburban environs, and the aforementioned sewer systems. As we are ostensibly intelligent, those in the fifth category are primary candidates to be banned, since fouling our own nests is monumentally stupid. "A responsible human society bans the use of resources which permanently reduce yields of sustainable resources, e.g. pollutants, persistent poisons, radioactives, large areas of concrete, and sewers from city to sea."[34] To do otherwise is to invite the failure of society. Consider the use of certain pesticides and other chemicals. Bayer and Syngenta sued the European Union because it banned neonicotinoids, which are linked to killing bee populations.[35] For these two companies (like Monsanto, Dow, BASF and others), anything that infringes on their right to a profit should be illegal, even if what they make a profit from is clearly detrimental to the ecosystemic actions that perpetuate life. It would be difficult to have a more monumentally short sighted and delusional ideology.

Our focus now shifts to Holmgren's twelve principles of permaculture with a brief discussion of each principle. The principles that Holmgren has developed inform the work of permaculture designers as they engage with the full design process.[36] "These principles are as universal, although the methods used to express them will vary greatly according to the place and situation. They are applicable to our personal, economic, social and political reorganisation as illustrated in Holmgren's permaculture flower."[37] The twelve principles are:

- Observe and interact with nature

- Catch and store energy

- Obtain a yield

---

34. Mollison, *Permaculture,* 17.

35. The New York Times, "Bee Survival in Europe." This is only one such case, there are many others.

36. A detailed discussion of the design process is beyond the scope of this chapter. For a more details see chapter three of Mollison's *Permaculture: A designer's manual;* Jacke and Toensmeier, *Edible Forest Gardens:* vol. 2.

37. Holmgren, "Permaculture Design Principles." The permaculture flower is featured on the website.

- Apply self-regulation and accept feedback
- Use and value renewable resources and services
- Produce no waste
- Design from patterns to details
- Integrate rather than segregate
- Use small and slow solutions
- Use and value diversity
- Use edges and value the marginal
- Creatively use and respond to change

Observe and interact with nature is straightforward. If a cultivated ecosystem is to be designed, then one must be in relationship with nature, and for the system to be effective, "careful observation and thoughtful interaction to reduce the need for both repetitive manual labor and for non-renewable energy high technology,"[38] is necessary. Low-tech solutions are favorable to high-tech ones because of the energy, materials, and waste involved in high-tech systems. We are likely, without some new, non-polluting, renewable energy source, facing what ecologist Howard Odum called a time of "energy descent."[39] That is, cheap fossil fuel energy is soon to be a thing of the past due to dwindling supplies and the need to dramatically reduce carbon in the atmosphere. For these reasons, we must learn to do with less of it. Careful observation of nature can give us new perspectives and the knowledge needed to address the problems associated with climate change, social dysfunction, and dwindling oil resources,[40] as well as the need to replace coal[41] and natural gas with cleaner alternatives,[42] along with the issues of toxic wastes and outdated nuclear power plants.[43]

Most of us are out of practice at this. "The development of good observation skills takes time and a quiet-centered condition. This also requires

38. Holmgren, *Principles and Pathways*, 13.

39. Hopkins, "What Is 'Energy Descent'?"

40. Beattie, "Peak Oil."

41. Gross, "Big Economies Are Falling Out of Love with Coal."

42. Proponents of using natural gas as a clean burning fuel fail to mention the horribly pollutive nature of its extraction. Similar issues surround coal mining. See: Greenpeace, "Toxic Sludge Leaks Expose True Costs of Coal."

43. For decades the U.S. and other nuclear capable nations dumped nuclear waste into the ocean. See: Kozakiewicz, "The Disposal of Nuclear Waste into the World's Oceans."

a change from a lifestyle that is indoor, semi-nocturnal, and media dominated to one that is outdoor, mainly daytime, and nature-focused."[44] Our
world moves at break-neck pace and is dominated by screens and devices.
We need to learn to be in nature, and to learn to be still. As Zen Buddhist
monk, Thich Nhat Hanh has said, "Don't just do something, sit there,"[45] and
do it outside.

Catch and store energy entails a great deal more than installing solar panels. "This principle deals with the capture and long-term storage of
energy, that is savings and investment to build natural capital and human
capital."[46] Our society currently uses vastly more energy than it stores as
we burn through fossil fuels indiscriminately. This will not be possible in
a low energy world, and we need to "rediscover opportunities to harvest
and store immediately available (on-site) renewable energies and wasted
resources across our rural and urban landscapes and in our households
and local economies" which will create resilience in the face of "inevitable
disruptions to energy and resource supply lines."[47] As energy flows into a
system, in the form of water, solar, wind, as well as various nutrients, it is
the work of the designer to capture as much of it and store it in the landscape for use in the home, workspaces, and soil. Strategies include using
wind and sun to season fuel wood, dry clothes, or for dehydrating foods.
Passive solar design elements, like having a south facing greenhouse, can
capture energy in the form of plants grown out of season to be eaten.[48]
With enough wind, there can be on-site power generation[49] and windmills
to pump water. Trees grown for timber capture solar energy, store carbon,
and can be used for fuel and lumber with proper management techniques
such as careful species selection, coppicing, and pollarding.[50]

44. Holmgren, *Principles and Pathways*, 16.

45. Valentine and Nhat Hanh, "101 Inspiring Mindfulness Quotes to Live By."

46. Holmgren, *Principles and Pathways*, 27.

47. Holmgren, *Principles and Pathways*, 29.

48. Coleman, *Four-Season Harvest*.

49. Average wind speeds need to be a minimum of 9.8–11.5 m.ph. for wind power
generation. See: eXtension, "Wind Energy for Homeowners, Farmers and Small
Businesses."

50. Coppicing is done to create new woody growth of certain trees and shrubs by cutting it down to a stump. This creates new growth of uniform size for fire wood, poles, and
other wood products. Regrowth is much faster than starting a new tree or shrub. Britain
was once famous for its coppice groves and are now starting to regrow them. Pollarding
is to cut the tree or shrub higher off of the ground to encourage regrowth. See: Jacke and

Empires have fallen because of degraded soils and much of America's soils (as well as soil globally) is now degraded due to industrial agriculture, erosion, and runoff.[51] Fortunately, soil has evolved to "catch and store plant nutrients in non-soluble but available forms.[52] We can replenish soils through composting food and yard "wastes" such as all of the immensely valuable leaves that fall each autumn that are then put in bags and hauled away. Timber and fuel forests need to be replanted on marginal land that is ill suited for agriculture in order to not only replenish soil, but also to remove carbon from the atmosphere. Tree planting is of paramount importance to the planet[53] and for permaculturists for this reason, as is rebuilding of the humus of the planet's agricultural soils and rangelands, which also store carbon in the soil and roots of perennial plants. "The differences between soils in their capacity to store water, nutrients and carbon is the greatest single factor in the productivity of terrestrial ecosystems and agriculture."[54]

When energy is captured and stored mindfully, we can obtain the yields necessary for the furtherance of life and the maintenance of systems. "This principle reminds us that we should design for self-reliance at all levels (including ourselves) [because without useful yields] whatever we design and develop will wither while elements that do generate immediate yield will proliferate."[55] No one can survive, much less work, on a stomach that is often empty. For this reason, beginning with redesigning our food system to one that is more local, less energy intensive, as well as being more diverse and nutrient dense is of utmost importance. Equally important is recreating fuel wood forests with coppice groves for heating and cooking needs. The residual effects of doing these two things alone are huge in terms of regeneration of soils, building community, and lessening dependence on fossil fuels. "Growing our food can give us aesthetic delight and relaxation,

---

Toensmeier, *Edible Forest Gardens*, vol. 1, 350, 354. For an extensive list of coppice species see Jacke and Toensmeier *Edible Forest Gardens*, Vol 2, 523–527.

51. For more on the soil crisis facing the U.S. see: Montgomery, *Dirt: The Erosion of Civilizations*.

52. Holmgren, *Principles and Pathways*, 34–35.

53. Trees are the lungs of our planet and deforestation, particularly in the Amazon rainforest, is driving climate change. Much of the Amazonian deforestation is done to create monocrops of commodity crops that go to feed cattle and chickens to supply fast food restaurants. See: Vidal, "The 7,000 km Journey That Links Amazon Destruction to Fast Food."

54. Holmgren, *Principles and Pathways*, 36–37.

55. Holmgren, *Principles and Pathways*, 56.

a better understanding of how nature works, a greater sense of security and well-being, and an appreciation of farmers who earn their living growing food...if we enjoy abundant, high-quality harvests, this will sustain us once the novelty has worn off and through the inevitable seasonal ups and downs."[56] Converting all those acres of lawns to food and fuel production would be a great way to transform suburbia from an energy drain to abundantly yielding organic food and fuel systems where neighbors get to know one another and work together.

The things that we do in our lifetime continue to affect our neighbors for generations to come, which is why the Iroquois made decisions based on how something would impact people seven generations[57] and the Bible speaks of the sins of the fathers being visited on children to the fourth generation.[58] For this reason, we must apply the Holmgren's fourth principle to our designs and lives in general, that is to apply self-regulation and accept feedback. In the industrialized world, we have done this poorly. "In modern society, we take for granted an enormous degree of dependence on large-scale, often remote, systems for the provision of our needs, while expecting a huge degree of freedom in what we do without external control. In a sense, our whole society is like a teenager who wants to have it all, have it now, without consequences."[59] While consuming resources and energy mindlessly, we have too often failed to notice the obvious feedback which results from our affluenza, such as acid rain, smog, dying coral reefs, nearly ceaseless international conflicts, and humanitarian crises that occur around the world. Self-control is an important evolutionary mechanism in biological entities that helps ensure survival of species,[60] yet we are not exercising it readily enough.

Effectively designed systems too can become more self-reliant,[61] such as kitchen gardens or diversely designed forest gardens and woodlots. Our own survival is not the only end we are trying to achieve, rather as permaculturists, we are striving to foster all life in a regenerative manner. "The more we come to depend on our own and local resources, the more likely we are to recognise problems and institute corrective behaviours to deal

---

56. Holmgren, *Principles and Pathways*, 61.

57. Joseph, "What Is the Seventh Generation Principle?"

58. Exodus 20:5; 34:7; Numbers 14:18; Deuteronomy 5:9

59. Holmgren, *Principles and Pathways*, 71.

60. Holmgren, *Principles and Pathways*, 73.

61. Holmgren, *Principles and Pathways*, 74.

with them."[62] This will take both individual action and a cultural revolution. Permaculture is "concerned with facilitating individuals, households, and local communities in increasing self-reliance and self-regulation."[63]

To do so, we as individuals need to connect deeply with our choices[64] as well as uncover patterns we may be blind to. Holmgren's self-audit process, provides people with a means of uncovering and connecting. To do this self-audit one can: brainstorm and list all of one's needs, wants, talents and skills, responsibilities, and addictions; make connections with everything that influences day to day life and choices made, map personal movement patterns, as well as the energy and material that flows to make them happen, take personal responsibility without blaming others or wallowing in guilt, identify the easiest opportunities for reducing dependence, doing less harm to one's neighbors and the planet, while improving your quality of life, then make small changes as time goes on and review the audit regularly.[65] This can be a somewhat daunting and humbling process. For example, if I seriously identify my addictions, I realize that my addiction to on-demand electricity and internet access, which I use for entertainment, academic work, and sometimes to just pass the time, is all contributing to my own outsized carbon footprint. Societally, we are hitting ourselves in the thumb with a hammer and failing to accept the feedback that doing it hurts, so we hit our thumbs over and over again.

As has been shown, we are spending our natural capital[66] at an alarming rate, along with depleting fossil and nuclear fuel sources, often for things which provide no inherent yield. "Spending our capital assets for day-to-day living is unsustainable in anyone's language. Permaculture design should aim to make best use of renewable natural resources to manage and maintain yields, even if the use of some non-renewable resources is needed to establish the system."[67] At my first Permaculture Design Course (PDC), Albert Bates[68], a former environmental lawyer turned permacul-

---

62. Holmgren, *Principles and Pathways*, 75.

63. Holmgren, *Principles and Pathways*, 79–80.

64. Cruz, "Connecting with Our Choices."

65. Holmgren, *Principles and Pathways*, 85–86.

66. For more on natural capital see: World Forum on Natural Capital, "What Is Natural Capital?"

67. Holmgren, *Principles and Pathways*, 93.

68. Bates, "Carbon Drawdown Sequestration with Biochar Bioeconomics." See also: Bates, "The Great Change."

turist and ecovillage designer, said that we must use the remaining fossil fuel energy wisely to establish new permaculture designed systems rather than continuing to use them as we have been.[69] That is a tough sell to oil companies, retailers, and corporations whose existence is predicated upon conspicuous consumption.

A good permaculture example of using a renewable resource is to use animals for preparing gardens or croplands for cultivation. Chickens placed in a mobile cage will scratch up all the weeds, grasses, and other plants in their search for bugs, worms, and seeds to eat, leaving freshly weeded, fertilized, and aerated soil behind. A gas-powered tiller is not necessary. Similarly, pigs will clean up a garden or annual crop plot quickly and can also be used in managed woodlots and forest gardens to clear brush, turn soil, eat seeds, and provide nutrient rich fertilizer to the soil. "In a similar way we can think of grazing animals as mowers, and plants as water and nutrient pumps, shelter and living fences. Living soil can be thought of as a filter, purifier, and sore of water and nutrients. Streams, swamps, and other waterways can be self-purifying water storages."[70] Likewise, there will always be some byproducts of our food preparation that can be turned into compost using worms to create rich vermicompost as they eat the vegetable matter and then excrete worm castings.[71]

Each week a large truck goes through the neighborhood picking up the detritus of American consumer culture. I am frequently astonished at the amount of garbage and recycling that people put out, myself included, to be taken to the local landfill because we live in a disposable culture. Holmgren's challenge in principle number six is to "produce no waste." Nature cycles everything it produces through the ecosystems. Humanity does not because of our current economic model is predicated on perpetual growth driven by over-consumption.[72] "This principle brings together traditional values of frugality and care for material goods, the mainstream concern about pollution, and the more radical perspective that sees wastes as resources and opportunities."[73] Recently, I came across a group of people turning plastic "waste" into new tools and other useful items with simple

---

69. Bates also called modern day humanity, "Hairless apes on the gas-crack of history."

70. Holmgren, *Principles and Pathways*, 102.

71. Gershuny and Langer, *Compost, Vermicompost, and Compost Tea.* See also: Appelhof, *Worms Eat My Garbage.*

72. Holmgren, *Principles and Pathways*, 113.

73. Holmgren, *Principles and Pathways*, 111.

machines which they had designed. They made the plans for the do-it-yourself machines open source so anyone can put their plans to use and set up a recycling/repurpose shop in their local community.[74] This is the essence of producing no waste, as well as bottom up action.[75]

Applying the 5 R's – refuse, reduce, reuse, repair, and recycle, gives us a "hierarchy of strategies for dealing with waste."[76] Our individual choices matter a great deal in the supply and demand economy. We do not have to buy all of the things being advertised, nor do we have to dispose of the things we have so readily. The cycle of overconsumption and the waste it produces must end with those of us in affluent countries and new habits of finding ways to creatively reuse old consumer goods, tools, and clothes must also brought back into fashion. New skills at repairing our computers, tablets, smartphones, appliances, and other items which took a great deal of energy to manufacture need to be developed and implemented, and then we as people paying attention to these matters can choose to give our custom to those practicing those skills. In this vein, a "Repair Café" has begun to actively resist throw-away culture in the United Kingdom thus giving new life to previously broken items.[77] Recycling of waste should be our last resort because it takes a great deal of energy to "actively degrade a material to its more basic constituents."[78] It is better to recycle than to throw something away, however.

Principle seven is to design from patterns to details. "The commonality of patterns observable in nature and society allows us to not only make sense of what we see but also to use a pattern from one context and scale to design in another."[79] The application of this principle is done as part of a site analysis. Patterns that a permaculturist will look for include: identifying the climate zone and its characteristics,[80] what kind of soil is on site,[81] what are the sources for energy flows such as solar, wind, and running water and

74. Precious Plastic, "Precious Plastic."
75. Holmgren, *Principles and Pathways,* 79–82.
76. Holmgren, *Principles and Pathways,* 112–115.
77. Lyons, "The Repair Cafes Waging War on Throwaway Culture."
78. Holmgren, *Principles and Pathways,* 115.
79. Holmgren, *Principles and Pathways,* 127.
80. ISC Audubon, "The Köppen Climate Classification System."
81. U.S. Food and Drug Administration, "Web Soil Survey."

where do they flow on-site, where are the watershed boundaries,[82] are there slopes and aspects to consider, what types of biomass are currently grown onsite such as trees, shrubs, and other plants, and how is human energy spent and where does it flow on site.[83] It takes a good deal of observation and research to do this type of site analysis.

Creating a zone map will enable the designer to place design elements within the design in areas where energy used to utilize and maintain them efficiently. Zones move from 0 (our homes as well as ourselves) up to Zone 5. "Permaculture zones are more-or-less concentric areas of intensity of use, which describe the power and efficiency of people working from the focal point (a dwelling). The closer to the centre, the more efficient and intensive is our use of the land; the farther away we go, the more we must rely on self-maintaining elements that require little input from us, and generally yield less for us."[84] I include human beings as part of Zone 0, because we need to know ourselves, our strengths and weaknesses, our personalities, skills, and how we learn and process information, as well as what may trigger us, in order to effectively live in community with others with minimal conflict.[85]

The following zonal recommendations are from Mollison.[86] Zone 1 is where people will be closest to the house/workspace because elements there will need to be observed frequently, harvested from and maintained, and visited more often. Here is where designers place water catchment, kitchen gardens, nests for egg laying chickens, culinary herbs, and if possible other livestock such as rabbits, worms, pigeons, fish, and guinea pigs. Zone 2 is managed, though less intensely than 1, and may contain orchards, small ponds, terraced areas, ranging animals, and their shelters. The farm zone is in Zone 3, where broadacre crops are grown and animals are pastured. Other elements may include hedgerows, barns, and larger water storage

82. NRCS, New Hampshire, "How to Read a Topographic Map and Delineate a Watershed."

83. To view an example of a permaculture design for a small scale farm with pictures of the water flow, zones, and current vegetation see my design project for the Advanced Permaculture Design Practicum I completed through Oregon State University, see Cruz, "Fiddle Creek Dairy Final Design."

84. Holmgren, *Principles and Pathways* 138.

85. As part of my process of understanding myself, I have taken multiple Myers-Briggs type indicator tests, engaged in therapy, and ascertained my learning style.
For resources related to self-awareness see: 16Personalities, "Free Personality Test." See also: Markova, *The Open Mind*.

86. Mollison, *Permaculture*, 49–51.

systems. Zone 4 is semi-wild but lightly managed and harvested from such as woodlots with unpruned, naturally occurring or intentionally planted trees and understory shrubs and plants.[87] Zone 5 is an unmanaged, wild area that, if it is entered at all, is done for observation purposes only. Some areas need to be left alone to function naturally. Not all sites will have all five zones. Many home-scale sites will only have 0–2. Every site is different and therefore "design techniques should be individually assessed for each situation and not adopted without thorough site analysis."[88]

The eighth principle defined by Holmgren is to integrate rather than segregate. Oftentimes our default mode of thinking is to segregate things from our lives or systems to prevent too much complexity. "The ability of the designer to create systems that are closely integrated depends on a broad view of the range of jigsaw-like lock-and-key relationships that character-ise ecological and social communities."[89] The more mature an ecosystem, the more likely one is to find mutualistic or symbiotic relationships rather than competitive ones.[90] Nature exhibits a wide range of relationships from predatory, to mutualistic, parasitic, symbiotic, and avoidance.[91] By learn-ing how these relationships function, the designer can make use of these types of patterns into an integrated whole designed system with resilience and redundancies built into the system.

An important aspect of this process of integration is incorporating ele-ments that serve more than one function, or "stacking functions" in perma-culture lingo. The dandelion illustrates this principle perfectly. In America, lawn and garden companies would have us eradicate this "weed" with toxic chemicals to maintain a monocropped lawn. This is short sighted in the ex-treme because the dandelion stacks functions incredibly well. The taproot of the dandelion penetrates deeply into soil allowing oxygen to reach the aerobic bacteria that need it to thrive as well as breaking up hardpan soil that is low in nutrients. It also has medicinal properties as a diuretic[92] and

87. For an explanation of forest architecture see Jacke and Toensmeier, *Edible Forest Gardens*, Vol 1, p 69–109. Knowing this architecture allows designers to intentionally mimic a forest thus creating yields from all the various layers by introducing and estab-lishing different species from the soil to the canopy.

88. "Millison Interview," email interview by author, March 16, 2018.

89. Holmgren, *Principles and Pathways* 155.

90. Holmgren, *Principles and Pathways*, 167

91. Holmgren, *Principles and Pathways*, 156–158.

92. Clare, Conroy, and Spelman, "The Diuretic Effect in Human Subjects of an Ex-tract of Taraxacum Officinale Folium over a Single Day,"

is dried and used as a coffee substitute.[93] The young greens are highly nutritious and add a tasty, slight bitterness to salads or can be sautéed in oil or boiled.[94] Likewise, the flowers are also edible[95] and can be made into wine as well; but more importantly they are one of the first flowers to emerge in the spring and therefore are an important source of food for pollinators as winter fades and the bees and other pollinating insects emerge.[96] The flowers also have a lovely delicate smell and when they go to seed children love to blow them into the wind, thus providing much needed brief moments of happiness, that also propagates this important pollinator plant. That is quite the list of yields and functions from a so-called weed. Integrating rather than segregating this plant provides a wealth of benefits to a design site in a similar way that practicing intentional diversity in our personal lives and communities does.[97]

Principle nine is countercultural, as is permaculture in general, in that it tells us to use small and slow solutions, rather than the current model of "get big or get out" in agriculture[98] or banks being deemed "too big to fail"[99] thus needing government bailouts. In permaculture design, however, designers work to ensure that the systems are designed to be functional at the smallest practical size to maximize energy efficiency. "The proverb "the bigger they are the harder they fall" is a reminder of one of the disadvantages of size and excessive growth. The proverb "slow and steady wins the race," is one of many ways to encourage patience while reflecting a common truth in nature and society."[100] A well designed and maintained garden perfectly exemplifies this principle due to their human scale, and

93. Schaefer, "7 Ways Dandelion Tea Could Be Good for You."

94. I personally prefer them lightly sautéed in bacon fat which is a traditional Pennsylvania Dutch preparation. If they are young and tender, I will use them in salads. Only forage for dandelion greens in places you know have not been chemically treated.

95. A naturalist at Lancaster County Park prepared dandelion flower fritters after an edible plant walk I participated in and they were delicious.

96. Bradbury, "Let Dandelions Grow."

97. bell hooks, in her book *Teaching Community,* writes that, "Hatred forms around the unknown, the difference of others." To break down these barriers in our society we must practice diversity in our relationships, cultural institutions, and communities. hooks, *Teaching Community,* 9.

98. Small scale farmers in America are often bought out to consolidate farms into fewer and fewer hands. See: Logsdon, *The Contrary Farmer.*

99. Investopedia, "Too Big to Fail."

100. Holmgren, *Principles and Pathways,* 81.

their capacity to yield abundant high-quality food, medicine, and culinary herbs, while also providing exercise, education, and connection to one's food. Further examples include, the mimicking forest architecture to take advantage of multiple vertical layers even in small spaces, low to medium density housing patterns, alternative economic models and currencies, and walking or biking instead of driving.[101]

Our world is shaped now by short term growth and profit forecasts that are heedless of a sustainable, much less regenerative future. This mentality affects agriculture, where growth hormones are fed to animals, GMO crops are increasingly grown, and even vegetable production techniques are used that make a quick harvest instead of nutrient density the goal. Even favoring annual crops (which do have a place in permaculture) over perennial ones is a sign of faster, more energy intensive production. In timber production as well, we see the need for speed mentality that favors fast growing, single species stands, rather than long rotation forestry of multiple species.[102] All of this is to our detriment as a society and to the ecology of the planet. Natural systems provide us with excellent working models of small and slow solutions. "The evidence that 'small is beautiful' and 'slow is sane' is all around us. The more we come to terms with peak energy and descent, the more we can recognise giant systems as dinosaurs of the era of fossil-fuel abundance. As we accept our own fallibility and mortality and tune into nature's patterns, we see that slow and steady does win the race."[103]

We live in a culture that in many ways as become homogeneous. One could be dropped off in almost any town in the U.S. and see the sameness of our culture with the ubiquitous fast-food and corporate chain restaurants, shopping malls, big box stores, and multiple lanes of traffic going to these places. Or we may be dropped off in a rural area and see nothing put corn or soybeans planted for seemingly miles all around. It seems as though uniqueness and diversity are unwelcome. In permaculture design, the opposite is the case, as espoused in principle ten – use and value diversity. "Diversity needs to be seen as a result of the balance and tension in nature between variety and possibility on one hand, and productivity and power on the other."[104] Putting all of our eggs in one basket can result in nothing

---

101. Holmgren, *Principles and Pathways*, 183.

102. Holmgren, *Principles and Pathways*, 192–197.

103. Holmgren, *Principles and Pathways*, 200.

104. Holmgren, *Principles and Pathways*, 203.

but a huge mess, particularly if those "eggs" are large scale systems driven by fossil fuel consumption.

Even in systems where there is one predominant tree species for example, there is still diversity present from the soil layer to the understory, though on a smaller scale than more diverse ecosystems. Increased diversity leads to fewer competitive relationships and more cooperation between species. "Diversity provides alternative pathways for essential ecosystem functions in the face of changing conditions. This makes sense from our understanding of traditional organisation of human systems, where diversity of crops and resources provides insurance against failure in one or another function."[105] As our planetary ecosystems evolve due to climate change we will need to put the principles and ethics of permaculture into practice as we redesign communities, food-ways, economies, and interpersonal interactions in order to be as resilient as possible.[106] "A deep respect for both natural and human diversity seems part of the wisdom in most spiritual traditions...A reference to this principle, and ultimately to the Care of the Earth ethic that requires us to consider and care for all of nature's diversity, can help us find the right balance."[107] In so doing we become more connected to our local bioregions, and all of its human inhabitants, as well as the flora and fauna, and create "cultures of place" in face of our globalized "culture of no-place."[108]

In places where two ecosystems come together, there is something called an ecotone, and in these ecotones is where diversity is often the very highest.[109] Think for example, of estuaries, places where freshwater flows into a body of salt water, as an example of a highly diverse ecotone. This mixing of two types of water creates a unique habitat with niches to be filled by different species. From this natural pattern comes the eleventh principle in Holmgren's list – use edges and value the marginal. These natural edges are unlike the arbitrary borders on maps, rather they meander and become either thicker or thinner in different spots. When we design more edge effect into a system, we create more niches for higher biodiversity, with the hope of obtaining more yields in a beautiful and stimulating landscape.[110]

105. Holmgren, *Principles and Pathways*, 205.

106. Holmgren, *Principles and Pathways*, 207.

107. Holmgren, *Principles and Pathways*, 215.

108. Holmgren, *Principles and Pathways*, 220.

109. Holmgren, *Principles and Pathways*, 224.

110. Mollison, *Permaculture*, 77.

"This principle reminds us to maintain awareness and make use of edges and margins at all scales and all systems."[111] Our communities often seek this edge effect, but poor design based upon car culture leads to the edge being pushed further and further from cities creating urban sprawl.[112]

We see this principle in action in forest gardens where the various layers, previously mentioned, are intentionally designed after the pattern found in established woodlands and forests. Vertical edges from the below the surface of the soil, such as fungal mycelium which provides nutrients to various species and then fruits into mushrooms.[113] Then there are various types of ground covers, be they clumpers, runners, mat forming, or climbers;[114] the shrub and understory tree layer; and finally all the way up into the canopy of the overstory. There, tall fruit and nut bearing trees can all create habitat, medicine, food for people and animals, as well as timber, cordage, and other useful biomass. In gardens, permaculturists create edge using rows that resemble a slithering snake rather than a straight line, or perhaps create more edge by using companion planting[115] with varieties of plants that enhance the growth of a companion plant, attract beneficial insects, or repel pests. Raised beds and contour plantings are also examples of using more edge. Planting trees and shrubs on marginal lands unfit for gardens or broadacre crops increases both edge and values the marginal.

In the Clint Eastwood film, *Heartbreak Ridge*, Eastwood's character, Gunnery Sergeant Highway is seen as a relic of a bygone era, what we in the Marines called, "Old Corps" in a sort of misguided nostalgia for a time that was tougher, and more black and white. One of Highway's favorite expressions in the film is to tell his squad of Marines to "Improvise, adapt, and overcome."[116] This expression encapsulates the twelfth and final principle from Holmgren which is to creatively use and respond to change. "This principle has two threads: designing to make use of change in a deliberate and cooperative way, and creatively responding or adapting to large-scale

---

111. Holmgren, *Principles and Pathways*, 23.

112. Holmgren, *Principles and Pathways*, 230.

113. For more details on the amazing world of mycelium and fungi see: Stamets, *Mycelium Running*.

114. Jacke and Toensmeier, *Edible Forest Gardens Vol 2*, 550.

115. For more on companion planting and organic vegetable gardening see: Denckla, *The Gardener's A–Z Guide to Growing Organic Food*.

116. *Heartbreak Ridge*

system change that is beyond our control or influence."[117] As has been shown in the previous chapters and in the aforementioned principles of permaculture, there are forces at play beyond the scope of our control and many are detrimental to the health and wellbeing of our neighbors and to the biosphere itself. Permaculture design is one set of tools that when properly implemented provides us with a creative platform to respond to changing economic conditions, climate change, and energy descent. As the practicing Buddhist knows, everything is impermanence.

Nature is our blueprint for responding to changes, and the observation skills learned by applying the first principle (observe and interact with nature) will help in responding creatively to our increasingly unstable climate. Learning the dynamics of succession "is essential to working with plants and land."[118] Identifying what the pioneer species are and which trees in some woods are climax species; knowing whether or not fire ecology plays a role in local ecosystems and what other types of ecosystem disturbances are prevalent on site, such as periodic flooding, gap dynamics in forests, or even grazing livestock used in rotational grazing systems are all important for the permaculture designer to know. With this knowledge and the knowledge that we are in the midst of unprecedented changes, we can design resilient, regenerative systems that provide fuel, food, fiber, and fodder along with yields for the soil, for pollinators, birds, mammals and aquatic life to flourish. "In any case, the forces at work are clearly beyond human control, so we might as well get on doing what we can to create a world that reflects human values and ethics within the constraints of nature's laws."[119]

117. Holmgren, *Principles and Pathways*, 239.
118. Holmgren, *Principles and Pathways*, 246.
119. Holmgren, *Principles and Pathways*, 266.

Conclusion

OUR PLANET IS IN a crisis that is largely of our own making due to rapacious consumption of fossil fuel resources; a failed capitalistic economic system that concentrates wealth into fewer and fewer hands; and a poorly designed agricultural model predicated upon easy access to diesel fuel, gasoline, oil, large equipment, and monocrops maintained in artificially constructed chemically soaked ecosystems. That is coupled with the individual car usage that clogs our roads and pollutes our skies. We're covering our planet in the garbage of our disposable culture and plastics are forming islands in our oceans as well as being eaten by or ensnaring aquatic life. Nuclear capable nations threaten our very existence as research and development is put towards weapons of ever greater destructive capacity in order to maintain geopolitical power. Climate change is proceeding at an alarming pace, with temperatures in the Arctic going above freezing during this winter season.[1] Our global society is in need of restructuring in both top down and bottom up ways and our local communities need this as well.

In this book, it has been my intention to show that by applying a basic principle of every global faith – what Christians call the Golden Rule, along with the Judeo-Christian ideal of loving one's neighbor as oneself, in conjunction with the ethics of permaculture design, that we will have some hope in creating a more egalitarian, peaceful, and sustainable world. We can start with our individual behaviors, shopping habits-be they for foodstuffs, clothing, or electronics, and the things we use and to maintain our homes and yards if we have them. Making these types of changes can make a big impact not only in our own microworld of home and neighborhood, but in the broader world as well, in a supply and demand type of economy.

1. Samenow, "North Pole Surges above Freezing in the Dead of Winter, Stunning Scientists."

This can also lead to top down change if we use the Golden Rule, along with the three ethics of permaculture, Creation Care, Neighbor Care, and Future Care, in our political decisions in terms of local, state, and federal elections. We are currently seeing the results of low voter turnout caused by apathy and voter suppression as well as fear-based rhetoric that intentionally seeks to divide and maintain white, patriarchal, capitalist privilege. The Trump administration is doing all it can to roll back civil rights for people of color, LGBTQIA people, immigrants, and people of faiths other than Christian. The saber rattling and war mongering have increased as well. It is clear that the Golden Rule, love of neighbor, and Creation Care, Neighbor Care, and Future Care, are not being heeded, perhaps now more than ever.

Whereas the world's faith traditions have given us the Golden Rule as a guiding religious or spiritual principle, permaculture design provides us with a secular framework that can be used by individuals as well as community organizations, or even urban planners to use to design resilient and regenerative systems. The tools do not provide a "one size fits all" template for cookie cutter style designs, but they are applicable across various bioregions, cultures, and ecosystems.[2] Nature, along with traditional indigenous cultures, has informed permaculture theory and practice. What is needed is for millions to learn these skills in local communities and apply them, sharing knowledge, paying it forward where possible, to rebuild communities, regenerate soil, plant productive tree-based systems, while dismantling systems of oppression, exclusion, and ecological destruction. There is much work to do and many hands make for lighter work, so let us work together.

2. See Mollison *Permaculture,* chapters 10, 11, 12, and 14 for more information on permaculture design in different climate conditions.

Bibliography

350.org. "A Global Campaign to Confront the Climate Crisis." Accessed January 18, 2018. https://350.org/.

Adaskaveg, James. "Major Post-Harvest Disease of California Citrus and Their Management." CalCitrusQuality.org. Accessed February 7, 2018. http://calcitrusquality.org/wp-content/uploads/2009/05/Adaskaveg-Citrus-3-11a.pdf.

Ahmed, Nafeez. "Iraq Invasion Was about Oil | Nafeez Ahmed." The Guardian. March 20, 2014. Accessed March 07, 2018. https://www.theguardian.com/environment/earth-insight/2014/mar/20/iraq-war-oil-resources-energy-peak-scarcity-economy.

Albers, Kyle, Peter Canepa, and Jennifer Miller. "Analyzing the Environmental Impact of Simple Shoes: A Life Cycle Assessment of the Supply Chain and Evaluation of End-of-Life Management Options," Donald Bren School of Environmental Science and Management. March 21, 2008. Accessed February 6, 2018. A Life Cycle Assessment of the Supply Chain and Evaluation of End-of-Life Management Options.

Amato, Nicole. "A Lack of Resources for Many Classrooms." The New York Times. March 26, 2015. Accessed February 16, 2018. https://www.nytimes.com/roomfordebate/2015/03/26/is-improving-schools-all-about-money/a-lack-of-resources-for-many-classrooms. American Psychological Association. "Incarceration Nation." October 2014. Accessed February 16, 2018. https://www.apa.org/monitor/2014/10/incarceration.aspx.

Amelinckx, Andrew. "Where Has All the Water Gone? Ogallala Aquifer Depletion." Modern Farmer. May 10, 2016. Accessed January 18, 2018. http://modernfarmer.com/2015/07/ogallala-aquifer-depletion/.

Appelhof, Mary. Worms Eat My Garbage. North Adams, MA: Storey, 2017.

Applewhite, J. Scott. "Enough Talk: Republicans Must Walk the Walk on Systemic Racism." - BostonGlobe.com. August 22, 2017. Accessed February 08, 2018. https://www.bostonglobe.com/opinion/2017/08/22/enough-talk-republicans-must-walk-walk-systemic-racism/lQTikOGNNlBdqup6EaJtBI/story.html.

Arenheim, Anna. "Israel Strikes 40 Hamas Targets over Two Weeks in Response to Rocket Fire." The Jerusalem Post | JPost.com. December 19, 2017. Accessed March 07, 2018. http://www.jpost.com/Arab-Israeli-Conflict/Second-Red-Alert-siren-heard-in-Hof-Ashkelon-Regional-Council-518341.

Associated Press. "Court rules North Carolina voter ID law unconstitutional." New York Post. July 30, 2016. Accessed February 15, 2018. https://nypost.com/2016/07/30/court-rules-north-carolina-voter-id-law-unconstitutional/.

Astore, William J. "Why It's Wrong to Equate Military Service with Heroism." The Huffington Post. July 22, 2010. Accessed March 09, 2018. https://www.huffingtonpost.com/william-j-astore/why-its-wrong-to-equate-m_b_655611.html.

BBC News. "Study: US is an Oligarchy, Not a Democracy." April 17, 2014. Accessed February 13, 2018. http://www.bbc.com/news/blogs-echochambers-27074746.

Banks, Jamie L. "National Emissions from Lawn and Garden Equipment." Environmental Protection Agency. September 2015. Accessed February 7, 2018. https://www.epa.gov/sites/production/files/2015-09/documents/banks.pdf.

Bates, Albert. "Carbon Drawdown Sequestration with Biochar Bioeconomics.". Accessed March 27, 2018. https://www.albertbates.cool/.

———. "The Great Change." The Great Change. March 25, 2018. Accessed March 27, 2018. https://peaksurfer.blogspot.com/.

Battaglin, William A. "Glyphosate Herbicide Found in Many Midwestern Streams, Antibiotics Not Common." Accessed January 18, 2018. https://toxics.usgs.gov/highlights/glyphosate02.html.

Ben & Jerry's. "rBGH." Accessed January 18, 2018. http://www.benjerry.com/values/issues-we-care-about/rbgh.

Beattie, Andrew. "Peak Oil." Investopedia. December 02, 2016. Accessed March 23, 2018. https://www.investopedia.com/terms/p/peak_oil.asp.

Begos, Kevin. "4 States Confirm Water Pollution from Drilling." USA Today. January 05, 2014. Accessed March 01, 2018. https://www.usatoday.com/story/money/business/2014/01/05/some-states-confirm-water-pollution-from-drilling/4328859/.

Belvedere, Matthew J. "Trump Reportedly Asks Why US Can't Use Nukes: MSNBC." CNBC. August 03, 2016. Accessed March 07, 2018. https://www.cnbc.com/2016/08/03/trump-asks-why-us-cant-use-nukes-msnbcs-joe-scarborough-reports.html.

Ben-Achour, Sabi. "What Do Stores Do with Unsold Merchandise?" Marketplace. March 10, 2014. Accessed February 6, 2018. https://www.marketplace.org/2014/03/10/business/ive-always-wondered/what-do-stores-do-unsold-merchandise.

Bender, Jeremy, Andy Kiersz, and Armin Rosen. "Some States Have Much Higher Enlistment Rates Than Others." Business Insider. July 20, 2014. Accessed March 07, 2018. http://www.businessinsider.com/us-military-is-not-representative-of-country-2014-7.

Berman, Ari. "Alabama, Birthplace of the Voting Rights Act, Is Once Again Gutting Voting Rights." The Nation. October 05, 2015. Accessed February 13, 2018. https://www.thenation.com/article/alabama-birthplace-of-voting-rights-act-once-again-gutting-voting-rights/.

Berman, Russell. "Kansas Republicans Sour on Their Tax-Cut Experiment." The Atlantic. February 24, 2017. Accessed February 13, 2018. https://www.theatlantic.com/politics/archive/2017/02/the-republican-blowback-against-sam-brownback-kansas/517641/.

Berry, Joshua. "Property Taxes & Public Education Funding: Inequality in the System." Academia.edu - Share research. Accessed February 16, 2018. https://www.academia.edu/912843/Property_Taxes_and_Public_Education_Funding_Inequality_in_the_System.

Bohn, T., M. Cuhra, and T. Traavik. "Compositional Differences in Soybeans on the Market: Glyphosate accumulates in Roundup Ready GM soybeans." Food Chemistry. December 18, 2013. Accessed January 18, 2018. http://www.sciencedirect.com/science/article/pii/S0308814613019201.

Boutsikirkis, *INHABIT: A Permaculture Perspective*. 2015. Accessed October 11, 2015. http://inhabitfilm.com/.

Bower, Jim. "Comparing the Ecological Footprints of America and the E.U." Swst. org. 2009. Accessed March 19, 2018. http://www.swst.org/wp/meetings/AM09/presentations/jbowyer_SWSTBoise2009.pdf.

Bradbury, Kate. "Let Dandelions Grow. Bees, Beetles and Birds Need Them." The Guardian. May 12, 2015. Accessed March 27, 2018. https://www.theguardian.com/lifeandstyle/gardening-blog/2015/may/12/dandelions-pollinators-wildlife-garden.

Brinlee, Morgan. "Obama Tweets to Parkland Students & His Message Will Empower You, Too." Bustle. February 23, 2018. Accessed March 07, 2018. https://www.bustle.com/p/obama-tweets-to-parkland-students-his-message-will-empower-you-too-8297964.

Britt, Lawrence. "The 14 Characteristics of Fascism." Ratical.org. 2003. Accessed March 07, 2018. https://ratical.org/ratville/CAH/fasci14chars.html.

Brown, Dee. *Bury My Heart at Wounded Knee: An Indian History of the American West*. New York, NY: Ishi, 2014.

Brown, Lynda. "The Roots of Your Health: Elaine Ingham on the Science of Soil." Sustainable Food Trust. March 6, 2015. Accessed January 18, 2018. http://sustainablefoodtrust.org/articles/roots-health-elaine-ingham-science-soil/.

Brunner, Daniel L., Jennifer L. Butler, and A. J. Swoboda. *Introducing Evangelical Ecotheology: Foundations in scripture, theology, history, and praxis*. Grand Rapids, MI: Baker Academic, 2014.

The Buddha. "The Dhammapada." Accessed March 07, 2018. http://pa56.org/ross/Buddha.htm.

Bump, Philip. "The New Congress Is 80 Percent White, 80 Percent Male and 92 Percent Christian." The Washington Post. January 05, 2015. Accessed February 08, 2018. https://www.washingtonpost.com/news/the-fix/wp/2015/01/05/the-new-congress-is-80-percent-white-80-percent-male-and-92-percent-christian/?utm_term=.e10051dfce29.

BusinessDictionary.com. "What is Natural Capital? Definition and Meaning." Accessed January 18, 2018. http://www.businessdictionary.com/definition/natural-capital.html.

Butler, Smedley. "War is a Racket." Ratical.org. Accessed February 28, 2018. https://ratical.org/ratville/CAH/warisaracket.pdf.

Calingaert, Daniel. "Rethinking U.S. Relations with Dictators." The Huffington Post. October 09, 2012. Accessed February 28, 2018. https://www.huffingtonpost.com/daniel-calingaert/rethinking-us-relations-w_b_1952077.html.

"Carlos Castillo Armas." Accessed February 28, 2018. http://www.radford.edu/~mpbaker/553People_and_Terms.htm.

Carlsen, Laura. "Under NAFTA, Mexico Suffered and the United States Felt its Pain." The New York Times. November 24, 2013. Accessed January 18, 2018. https://www.nytimes.com/roomfordebate/2013/11/24/what-weve-learned-from-nafta/under-nafta-mexico-suffered-and-the-united-states-felt-its-pain.

Cascadia Permaculture. "Jude Hobbs: Permaculture Design Courses and Teacher Trainings." 2013. Accessed March 23, 2018. http://cascadiapermaculture.com/.

Cattle Empire. "In the Heart of the Beef Feeding Empire | Satanta, KS." Accessed June 16, 2017. http://cattle-empire.net/.

Centers for Disease Control and Prevention. "Facts about Chlorine." Centers for Disease Control and Prevention. April 10, 2013. Accessed February 07, 2018. https://emergency.cdc.gov/agent/chlorine/basics/facts.asp.

———. "Phthalates Factsheet." Centers for Disease Control and Prevention. April 07, 2017. Accessed February 07, 2018. https://www.cdc.gov/biomonitoring/phthalates_factsheet.html.

Cetawayo, Ameerah. "How Much Money Does an Average Family Spend on Cleaning Products in a Year?" Budgeting Money. Accessed February 07, 2018.

Choi, Anna. "Impact of Fluoride on Neurological Development in Children." Harvard T.H. Chan School of Public Health. December 22, 2014. Accessed February 07, 2018. https://www.hsph.harvard.edu/news/features/fluoride-childrens-health-grandjean-choi/.

Cholia, Ami. "The Top 5 Reasons Why We Should Grow Hemp." The Huffington Post. August 06, 2009. Accessed February 06, 2018. http://www.huffingtonpost.com/2009/08/06/the-top-5-reasons-why-we_n_253348.html.

Chomsky, Noam. "Noam Chomsky: The Long, Shameful History of American Terrorism." In These Times. November 3, 2014. Accessed March 01, 2018. http://inthesetimes.com/article/17311/noam_chomsky_the_worlds_greatest_terrorist_campaign.

———. "Not Since the War of 1812." Truthout. September 13, 2011. Accessed March 09, 2018. http://www.truth-out.org/news/item/3276:not-since-the-war-of-1812.

Clare, B. A., R. S. Conroy, and K. Spelman. "The Diuretic Effect in Human Subjects of an Extract of Taraxacum Officinale Folium over a Single Day." Journal of Alternative and Complementary Medicine (New York, N.Y.). August 2009. Accessed March 27, 2018. https://www.ncbi.nlm.nih.gov/pubmed/19678785.

Clemente, Frank, Imara Salas, and Sarah Anderson. "Walmart's Executive Bonuses Cost Taxpayers Millions | IPS." Institute for Policy Studies. June 26, 2014. Accessed February 21, 2018. http://www.ips-dc.org/taxpayers_subsidize_walmart_execs/.

Coleman, Eliot. Four-season Harvest: Organic Vegetables from Your Home Garden All Year Long. White River Junction, VT: Chelsea Green, 1999.

Cone, James H. The Cross and the Lynching Tree. Maryknoll, NY: Orbis Books, 2016.

Cooper, William H. "Free Trade Agreements: Impact on U.S. Trade and Implications for U.S. Trade Policy." Congressional Research Service. February 26, 2014. Accessed February 6, 2018. https://fas.org/sgp/crs/row/RL31356.pdf.

Corasaniti, Nick. "Bernie Sanders Makes Rare Appeal to Evangelicals at Liberty University." The New York Times. September 14, 2015. Accessed February 08, 2018. https://www.nytimes.com/politics/first-draft/2015/09/14/bernie-sanders-makes-rare-appeal-to-evangelicals-at-liberty-university/.

Craffert, Pieter F. The Life of a Galilean Shaman: Jesus of Nazareth in Anthropological-Historical Perspective. Eugene: Cascade Books, 2008.

Crawford, Alex. "Meet Dorsen, 8, Who Mines Cobalt to Make Your Smartphone Work." Sky News. February 28, 2017. Accessed February 06, 2018. http://news.sky.com/story/meet-dorsen-8-who-mines-cobalt-to-make-your-smartphone-work-10784120.

Cressey, Daniel. "Widely Used Herbicide Linked to Cancer." Nature.com: International Weekly Journal of Science. March 24, 2015. Accessed February 07, 2018. http://www.nature.com/news/widely-used-herbicide-linked-to-cancer-1.17181.

Cruz, Dillon Naber. "Connecting with Our Choices." Creation Care, Neighbor Care, Future Care- The World through a Permaculture Lens. September 12, 2013. Accessed

March 23, 2018. https://dilloncruz72.wordpress.com/2013/12/09/connecting-with-our-choices/.

———. "Fiddle Creek Dairy Final Design." Creation Care, Neighbor Care, Future Care. "The World through a Permaculture Lens." November 17, 2015. Accessed March 27, 2018. https://dilloncruz72.wordpress.com/2015/03/20/fiddle-creek-dairy-final-design/.

Curl, Joseph. "Court Concedes DNC, Wasserman Schultz Rigged Primaries for Hillary." Daily Wire. August 27, 2017. Accessed February 11, 2018. https://www.dailywire.com/news/20271/court-admits-dnc-wasserman-schulz-rigged-primaries-joseph-curl.

Danielle, Britni. "Perspective | Sally Hemings Wasn't Thomas Jefferson's Mistress. She Was His Property." The Washington Post. July 07, 2017. Accessed February 15, 2018. https://www.washingtonpost.com/outlook/sally-hemings-wasnt-thomas-jeffersons-mistress-she-was-his-property/2017/07/06/db5844d4–625d-11e7–8adc-fea80e32bf47_story.html?utm_term=.a847dcdab7f0.

"Dave Jacke Interview." Telephone interview by author. March 19, 2018.

Davis, Kenneth C. *In the Shadow of Liberty: The Hidden History of Slavery, Four Presidents, and Five Black Lives*. Square Fish, 2018.

Defenders of Wildlife. "Basic Facts About Prairie Dogs." September 19, 2016. Accessed March 19, 2018. https://defenders.org/prairie-dog/basic-facts.

Deffeyes, Kenneth S. "Hubbert's Peak, The Peak." Princeton University. 2011. Accessed January 18, 2018. https://www.princeton.edu/hubbert/the-peak.html.

Democracy Now! "Bernie Blackout? As DNC Accused of Targeting Sanders, Corporate Media Ignores Historic Campaign." December 21, 2015. Accessed February 11, 2018. https://www.democracynow.org/2015/12/21/bernie_blackout_as_dnc_accused_of.

Denchak, Melissa. "The Dirty Fight over Canadian Tar Sands Oil." NRDC. December 31, 2015. Accessed March 01, 2018. https://www.nrdc.org/stories/dirty-fight-over-canadian-tar-sands-oil.

Denckla, Tanya L.K. *The Gardener's A-Z Guide to Growing Organic Food*. North Adams, MA: Storey, 2003.

Dengler, Roni. "Neonicotinoid Pesticides are Slowly Killing Bees." PBS. June 29, 2017. Accessed February 07, 2018. https://www.pbs.org/newshour/science/neonicotinoid-pesticides-slowly-killing-bees.

Department of Defense. "Fiscal Year 2017 Budget Request." Comptroller.defense.gov. February 9, 2016. Accessed March 7, 2018. http://comptroller.defense.gov/Portals/45/Documents/defbudget/fy2017/FY2017_Budget_Request.pdf.

———. "Population Representation in the Military Services: Fiscal Year 2014 Summary Report." CNA.org. 2014. Accessed March 7, 2018. https://www.cna.org/pop-rep/2014/summary/summary.pdf.

DeSilver, Drew. "5 Facts about the Minimum Wage." Pew Research Center. January 04, 2017. Accessed February 21, 2018. http://www.pewresearch.org/fact-tank/2017/01/04/5-facts-about-the-minimum-wage/.

Devega, Chauncey. "Peak Propaganda: Fox News Creates an Alternate Reality, Then CNN Perpetuates It." Salon. November 03, 2016. Accessed March 07, 2018. https://www.salon.com/2016/11/02/peak-propaganda-fox-news-creates-an-alternate-reality-and-cnn-perpetuates-it/.

Devereaux, Ryan. "The NFL, the Military, and the Hijacking of Pat Tillman's Story." The Intercept. September 28, 2017. Accessed March 07, 2018. https://theintercept. com/2017/09/28/pat-tillman-nfl-protest-death-army-disgrace/.

Dillinger, Jessica. "US Poverty Level by State." WorldAtlas. November 26, 2015. Accessed March 07, 2018. https://www.worldatlas.com/articles/us-poverty-rate-by-state.html.

Dingeman, Robbie. "Double-Decking Freeway among Lingle's Proposals." The Honolulu Advertiser | Hawaii's Newspaper. November 8, 2002. Accessed February 08, 2018. http://the.honoluluadvertiser.com/article/2002/Nov/08/ln/ln02a.html.

Doehring, Carrie. The Practice of Pastoral Care: A Postmodern Approach. Louisville, KY: Westminster John Knox, 2015.

Dolan, Maura, and Jaweed Kaleem. "U.S. 9th Circuit Court of Appeals Refuses to Reinstate Trump's Travel Ban." Los Angeles Times. June 12, 2017. Accessed February 11, 2018. http://www.latimes.com/local/lanow/la-na-9thcircuit-travel-ban-20170530-story. html.

Dole Plantation. "Dole Plantation: Hawaii's Complete Pineapple Experience." Accessed March 09, 2018. https://www.doleplantation.com/.

Donnelly, Thomas. "Rebuilding America's Defenses: Strategy, Forces and Resources for a New Century." Information Clearinghouse. September 2000. Accessed February 28, 2018. http://www.informationclearinghouse.info/pdf/RebuildingAmericasDefenses. pdf.

Dotinga, Randy. "Why America forgets the War of 1812." The Christian Science Monitor. June 08, 2012. Accessed March 09, 2018. https://www.csmonitor.com/Books/ chapter-and-verse/2012/0608/Why-America-forgets-the-War-of-1812.

Douglas-Bowers, Devon. "Slavery by Another Name: The Convict Lease System." The Hampton Institute. October 30, 2013. Accessed February 16, 2018. http://www. hamptoninstitution.org/convictleasesystem.html.

Duhigg, Charles. "Millions Drink Tap Water That Is Legal, but Maybe Not Healthy." The New York Times. December 16, 2009. Accessed February 07, 2018. http://www. nytimes.com/2009/12/17/us/17water.html.

Dwyer, Jim. "Where Unsold Clothes Meet People in Need." The New York Times. January 09, 2010. Accessed February 06, 2018. http://www.nytimes.com/2010/01/10/ nyregion/10about.html.

The Ecologist. "Glyphosate Found in Breast Milk." April 28, 2014. Accessed January 18, 2018. http://www.theecologist.org/News/news_analysis/2374941/glyphosate_ found_in_breast_milk.html.

Eddington, Patrick G. "Why Are FBI Agents Trammeling the Rights of Antiwar Activists?" Newsweek. April 21, 2016. Accessed February 28, 2018. http://www.newsweek.com/ why-are-fbi-agents-trammeling-rights-anti-war-activists-376759.

Eglash, Ruth. "Is Israel an 'Apartheid' State? This U.N. Report Says Yes." The Washington Post. March 16, 2017. Accessed March 07, 2018. https://www.washingtonpost.com/ news/worldviews/wp/2017/03/16/is-israel-an-apartheid-state-this-u-n-report-says-yes/?utm_term=.cae82154c3cf.

Eidenmuller, Michael E. "Martin Luther King, Jr: A Time to Break Silence (Declaration Against the Vietnam War)." American Rhetoric. Accessed March 09, 2018. http:// www.americanrhetoric.com/speeches/mlkatimetobreaksilence.htm. Speech delivered April 4, 1967.

Endocrine Society, Endocrine. "Phthalate, Environmental Chemical is Linked to Higher Rates of Childhood Obesity." ScienceDaily. June 2012. Accessed February 07, 2018. https://www.sciencedaily.com/releases/2012/06/120626113915.htm.

Environmental Working Group. "Consumer Guides." Environmental Working Group. Accessed February 07, 2018. http://www.ewg.org/consumer-guides.

Environmental Protection Agency. "When it's Hot." March 24, 2017. Accessed February 07, 2018. https://www.epa.gov/watersense/when-its-hot.

Epstein, Jennifer. "Clinton Says Giving Paid Speeches to Wall Street Firms a Mistake." Bloomberg.com. September 10, 2017. Accessed February 11, 2018. https://www.bloomberg.com/news/articles/2017–09–10/clinton-done-with-being-a-candidate-as-she-recalls-2016-errors.

eXtension. "Wind Energy for Homeowners, Farmers and Small Businesses." August 2, 2013. Accessed March 27, 2018. http://articles.extension.org/pages/26606/wind-energy-for-homeowners-farmers-and-small-businesses.

Fassihi, Farnaz. "The U.S. Is Still Iran's Great Satan." The Wall Street Journal. July 17, 2015. Accessed February 28, 2018. https://www.wsj.com/articles/the-u-s-is-still-irans-great-satan-1437170607.

Fifield, Anna. "Contractors Reap $138B from Iraq War." CNN. Accessed March 01, 2018. https://www.cnn.com/2013/03/19/business/iraq-war-contractors/index.html.

Fluoride Action Network. Accessed February 07, 2018. http://fluoridealert.org/.

Fox, Justin. "A Look Back at Bush's Economic Missteps." Time. January 19, 2009. Accessed February 06, 2018. http://content.time.com/time/specials/packages/article/0,28804,1872229_1872230_1872236,00.html.

Frantz, Barry. "Natural Resources Conservation Service." Ogallala Aquifer Initiative | NRCS. Accessed January 18, 2018. https://www.nrcs.usda.gov/wps/portal/nrcs/detailfull/national/programs/initiatives/?cid=stelprdb1048809.

Frieden, Tom. "Antibiotic Resistance Threats in the United States, 2013." U.S. Department of Health and Human Services. 2013. Accessed June 16, 2017.

Friedersdorf, Conor. "'Every Person Is Afraid of the Drones': The Strikes' Effect on Life in Pakistan." The Atlantic. September 25, 2012. Accessed March 01, 2018. https://www.theatlantic.com/international/archive/2012/09/every-person-is-afraid-of-the-drones-the-strikes-effect-on-life-in-pakistan/262814/.

Gammon, Crystal. "Weed-Whacking Herbicide Proves Deadly to Human Cells." Scientific American. June 23, 2009. Accessed January 18, 2018. https://www.scientificamerican.com/article/weed-whacking-herbicide-p/.

Gerrard, Jeremy. "High Levels of RoundUp in Soybeans." July 29, 2014. Accessed January 18, 2018. http://www.foodengineeringmag.com/articles/92552-high-levels-of-roundup-in-soybeans.

Gershuny, Grace, and Jocelyn Langer. Compost, Vermicompost, and Compost Tea: Feeding the Soil on the Organic Farm. White River Junction, VT: Chelsea Green 2011.

Ghose, Tia. "Why Is Water So Essential for Life?" LiveScience. September 29, 2015. Accessed February 07, 2018. http://www.livescience.com/52332-why-is-water-needed-for-life.html.

Ghosh, Bobby. "Who's Who on the CIA Payroll." Time. October 28, 2009. Accessed March 07, 2018. https://content.time.com/time/specials/packages/article/0,28804,1933053_1933052_1933051,00.html.

Gilens, Martin, and Benjamin I. Page. "Testing Theories of American Politics: Elites, Interest Groups, and Average Citizens." Scholar.Princeton.edu. September 9, 2014.

Accessed February 13, 2018. https://scholar.princeton.edu/sites/default/files/mgilens/files/gilens_and_page_2014_-testing_theories_of_american_politics.doc.pdf.

Gillam, Carey. "U.S. Researchers Find Roundup Chemical in Water, Air." Reuters. August 31, 2011. Accessed June 5, 2017. http://www.reuters.com/article/us-glyphosate-pollution-idUSTRE77U61720110831.

Given, Casey. "Milo Yiannopoulos and Richard Spencer Remind Us What Free Speech Is and Isn't." Rare. June 01, 2017. Accessed February 08, 2018. https://rare.us/rare-politics/getting-it-right/milo-yiannopoulos-and-richard-spencer-remind-us-what-free-speech-is-and-isnt/.

Glasmeir, Amy K., PhD. "A Calculation of the Living Wage." Living Wage Calculator. January 26, 2018. Accessed February 16, 2018. http://livingwage.mit.edu/articles/27-new-data-up-calculation-of-the-living-wage.

Global Footprint Network. "Ecological Footprint." Accessed March 19, 2018. https://www.footprintnetwork.org/our-work/ecological-footprint/.

———. "Ecological Wealth of Nations." 2017. Accessed March 19, 2018. http://www.footprintnetwork.org/content/documents/ecological_footprint_nations/.

Global Slavery Index "United States - Prevalence.". Accessed February 15, 2018. https://www.globalslaveryindex.org/country/united-states/.

———. "Unravelling the Numbers." Accessed February 15, 2018. https://www.globalslaveryindex.org/findings/.

Goodman, Amy, and Noam Chomsky. "'The Assad Regime is a Moral Disgrace': Noam Chomsky on Ongoing Syrian War." Democracy Now! April 5, 2017. Accessed February 28, 2018. https://www.democracynow.org/2017/4/5/the_assad_regime_is_a_moral.

Gordon-Reed, Annette. "The Jefferson Enigma- Blacks and the Founding Father." PBS. Accessed February 15, 2018. https://www.pbs.org/wgbh/pages/frontline/shows/jefferson/enigma/blacks.html.

Grace, Stephanie. "How Bobby Jindal Broke the Louisiana Economy." Newsweek. April 01, 2016. Accessed February 13, 2018. http://www.newsweek.com/how-bobby-jindal-broke-louisiana-economy-337999.

Grandin, Greg. "How America's 1989 Invasion of Panama Explains the Current US Foreign Policy Mess." Mother Jones. June 24, 2017. Accessed March 07, 2018. https://www.motherjones.com/politics/2014/12/our-forgotten-invasion-panama-key-understanding-us-foreign-policy-today/.

———. "Why Did the US Drop 26,171 Bombs on the World Last Year?" The Nation. January 15, 2017. Accessed February 11, 2018. https://www.thenation.com/article/why-did-the-us-dropped-26171-bombs-on-the-world-last-year/.

Grandin, Temple. "Dark Cutters (DFD)." Accessed June 16, 2017. http://www.grandin.com/meat/dkcut.html.

———. "Stress and Meat Quality." Accessed January 18, 2018. http://www.grandin.com/meat/meat.html.

Greenfield, Nicole. "The Dirt on Antibacterial Soaps." NRDC. December 15, 2016. Accessed February 07, 2018. https://www.nrdc.org/stories/dirt-antibacterial-soaps.

Greenpeace. "Toxic Sludge Leaks Expose True Costs of Coal." Greenpeace.org. January 12, 2009. Accessed March 23, 2018. https://www.greenpeace.org/archive-international/en/news/features/coal-ash-spills-expose-more-of/.

Greenwald, Glenn. "U.S. Admits Israel Is Building Permanent Apartheid Regime - Weeks After Giving It $38 Billion." The Intercept. October 06, 2016. Accessed March 07, 2018. https://theintercept.com/2016/10/06/u-s-admits-israel-is-building-permanent-apartheid-regime-weeks-after-giving-it-38-billion/.

Griffin, David Ray. "Can Civilization Survive the CO2 Crisis?" CNN. April 14, 2015. Accessed February 28, 2018. https://www.cnn.com/2015/01/14/opinion/co2-crisis-griffin/index.html.

Gross, Daniel. "Across the Globe, Big Economies Are Falling Out of Love with Coal." Slate Magazine. March 16, 2015. Accessed March 23, 2018. http://www.slate.com/articles/business/the_juice/2015/03/peak_coal_yes_the_u_s_and_other_big_economies_are_falling_out_of_love_with.html.

Grossman, Zoltan. "From Wounded Knee to Syria." Zoltan Grossman. Accessed March 07, 2018. https://sites.evergreen.edu/zoltan/interventions/.

Guelph University. "Biodiversity Helps Protect Nature against Human Impacts." ScienceDaily. February 6, 2013. Accessed February 07, 2018. https://www.sciencedaily.com/releases/2013/02/130206131052.htm.

Gussone, Felix, MD. "America's Obesity Epidemic Reaches Record High, New Report Says." NBCNews.com. October 13, 2017. Accessed February 07, 2018. https://www.nbcnews.com/health/health-news/america-s-obesity-epidemic-reaches-record-high-new-report-says-n810231.

Guynup, Sharon, and Nicolas Ruggia. "For Most People, Eating Bugs Is Only Natural." National Geographic. July 15, 2004. Accessed March 23, 2018. https://news.nationalgeographic.com/news/2004/07/0715_040715_tvinsectfood.html.

Hamilton, Keegan. "How Private Prisons Are Profiting from Locking up US Immigrants." VICE News. October 06, 2015. Accessed February 16, 2018. https://news.vice.com/article/how-private-prisons-are-profiting-from-locking-up-us-immigrants.

Harden, Blaine. "The U.S. War Crime North Korea Won't Forget." The Washington Post. March 24, 2015. Accessed March 09, 2018. https://www.washingtonpost.com/opinions/the-us-war-crime-north-korea-wont-forget/2015/03/20/fb525694-ce80-11e4-8c54-ffb5ba6f2f69_story.html?utm_term=.34d74fa6f4ca.

Hartmann, Thom. The Last Hours of Ancient Sunlight: Waking up to personal and global transformation. London: Hodder & Stoughton, 2001.

Hartung, William D. "Trump Is on His Way to Record-Setting Defense Spending in 2018." The Nation. January 11, 2018. Accessed February 13, 2018. https://www.thenation.com/article/trump-is-on-his-way-to-record-setting-defense-spending-in-2018/.

Heartbreak Ridge. Directed by Clint Eastwood. U.S, Warner Brothers, 1989.

Herbert, Bob. "In America; Nike's Pyramid Scheme." The New York Times. June 09, 1996. Accessed February 06, 2018. http://www.nytimes.com/1996/06/10/opinion/in-america-nike-s-pyramid-scheme.html.

Hetter, Katia. "Where Are the Worlds Happiest Countries?" CNN. March 21, 2017. Accessed February 06, 2018. http://www.cnn.com/2017/03/20/travel/worlds-happiest-countries-united-nations-2017/index.html.

The History Channel. "Americans Overthrow Hawaiian Monarchy." History.com. Accessed March 09, 2018. https://www.history.com/this-day-in-history/americans-overthrow-hawaiian-monarchy.

———."Sally Hemings." History.com. 2010. Accessed February 15, 2018. https://www.history.com/topics/sally-hemings.

Hobgood, Mary E. *Dismantling Privilege: An ethics of accountability*. Cleveland: United Church Press, 2000.

Holmgren, David. "Permaculture Design Principles." Permaculture Principles. Accessed March 21, 2018. https://permacultureprinciples.com/principles/.

———. David. *Permaculture: Principles and Pathways Beyond Sustainability*. Petersfield: Permanent, 2002.

Homestead Gardens. "List of Nitrogen Fixing Plants." Accessed February 7, 2018.

hooks, bell. *Teaching Community: A Pedagogy of Hope*. New York: Routledge, 2003.

Hopkins, Rob. "What Is 'Energy Descent'?" Transition Culture RSS. Accessed March 23, 2018. https://www.transitionculture.org/essential-info/what-is-energy-descent/.

Hoppe, Hans Wolfgang. "Determination of Glyphosate Residues in Human Urine Samples from 18 European Countries." June 12, 2013. Accessed July 6, 2017. https://www. foeeurope.org/sites/default/files/glyphosate_studyresults_june12.pdf.

Horovitz, Bruce. "Fast-Food Strikes Widen into Social-Justice Movement." USA Today. April 15, 2015. Accessed February 16, 2018. https://www.usatoday.com/story/ money/2015/04/15/fast-food-strike-fight-for-15-service-employees-international- union/25787045/.

Houry, Eimad. "World Poverty Quiz." Accessed February 07, 2018. https://leap.mercer. edu/poverty/world-poverty/.

Hoxie, Josh. "Blacks and Latinos Will Be Broke in a Few Decades." Fortune. September 19, 2017. Accessed March 07, 2018. http://fortune.com/2017/09/19/racial-inequality- wealth-gap-america/.

Hribar, Carrie. "Understanding Concentrated Animal Feeding Operations and their Impact on Communities." Center for Disease Control. 2010. Accessed July 16, 2017. https://www.cdc.gov/nceh/ehs/docs/understanding_cafos_nalboh.pdf.

Human Rights Watch. "US: Drug Arrests Skewed by Race." April 17, 2015. Accessed February 16, 2018. https://www.hrw.org/news/2009/03/02/us-drug-arrests-skewed- race.

Husband, Andrew. "Ex-White Supremacist Schools Megyn Kelly on Dog Whistles and Fox News." UPROXX. January 16, 2018. Accessed March 07, 2018. https://uproxx. com/news/megyn-kelly-dog-whistle-fox-news/.

Hutchinson, Alex. "Is Recycling Worth It? PM Investigates its Economic and Environmental Impact." Popular Mechanics. November 14, 2017. Accessed February 06, 2018. http://www.popularmechanics.com/science/environment/a3752/4291566/.

IMDb. "A State of Mind (2004)." Accessed March 07, 2018. http://www.imdb.com/title/ tt0456012/.

———. "The Day After (TV Movie 1983)." Accessed March 07, 2018. http://www.imdb. com/title/tt0085404/.

ISAAA.org. "Advanced Search: 331 events found." GM Approval Database Advanced Search. Accessed January 18, 2018. http://www.isaaa.org/gmapprovaldatabase/ advsearch/default.asp?CropID=Any&TraitTypeID=1&DeveloperID=Any&Countr yID=Any&ApprovalTypeID=Any

ISC Audubon. "The Köppen Climate Classification System | Resources." ISC-Audubon. Accessed March 27, 2018. http://www.thesustainabilitycouncil.org/resources/the- koppen-climate-classification-system/.

Ingham, Elaine. "Building Soil Health by Dr. Elaine Ingham." Honest Conversations on Business, Farming, Permaculture, and Life. 2014. Accessed January 18, 2018. http:// www.permaculturevoices.com/building-soil-health-by-dr-elaine-ingham-pvp096/.

Investopedia. "Too Big to Fail." February 22, 2018. Accessed March 28, 2018. https://www. investopedia.com/terms/t/too-big-to-fail.asp.

Jacke, Dave, and Eric Toensmeier. *Edible Forest Gardens: Ecological Design and Practice for Temperate-Climate Permaculture.* Vol. Vol. 1. 2 vols. White River Junction, VT: Chelsea Green, 2005.

———. *Edible Forest Gardens: Ecological Design and Practice for Temperate-Climate Permaculture.* Vol. 2. 2 vols. White River Junction, VT: Chelsea Green, 2005.

Johns, Tracy. "Keying in on Keystone Species." Ask a Biologist. November 06, 2009. Accessed March 19, 2018. https://askabiologist.asu.edu/explore/keying-keystone-species.

Joseph, Bob. "What Is the Seventh Generation Principle?" Indigenous Corporate Training Inc. May 29, 2012. Accessed March 21, 2018. https://www.ictinc.ca/blog/seventh-generation-principle.

Joseph, Brian. "Is 'Fragrance' Making Us Sick?" Mother Jones. February 1, 2016. Accessed February 7, 2018. http://www.motherjones.com/environment/2016/01/toxic-chemicals-fragrance-cosmetics-safety .

Juhasz, Antonia. "Why the War in Iraq Was Fought for Big Oil." CNN. April 15, 2013. Accessed February 06, 2018. http://www.cnn.com/2013/03/19/opinion/iraq-war-oil-juhasz/index.html.

Kamp, Karin. "Donald Trump and the Escalation of Hate." BillMoyers.com. June 15, 2016. Accessed February 08, 2018. http://billmoyers.com/story/donald-trump-escalation-hate/.

Kennedy, Paul M. *The Rise and Fall of the Great Powers: Economic change and military conflict from 1500 to 2000.* New York: Random House, 1988.

Kenny, Charles. "We're All the 1 Percent." Foreign Policy. February 26, 2012. Accessed February 06, 2018. https://foreignpolicy.com/2012/02/27/were-all-the-1-percent/.

Kimura, Donna. "How Much Do You Need to Earn to Afford a Modest Apartment?" Housingfinance.com. May 25, 2016. Accessed February 21, 2018. http://www. housingfinance.com/news/affordable-housing-eludes-americas-workers_o.

King, Erica Y. "Black Men Get Longer Prison Sentences than White Men for the Same Crime: Study." ABC News. November 17, 2017. Accessed February 16, 2018. http:// abcnews.go.com/Politics/black-men-sentenced-time-white-men-crime-study/ story?id=51203491.

King, Martin Luther, Jr. "I Have A Dream." RiseEarth. January 01, 1970. Accessed February 16, 2018. http://www.riseearth.com/2013/01/martin-luther-king-jr-i-have-dream. html.

Kingsolver, Barbara, Steven L. Hopp, and Camille Kingsolver. *Animal, Vegetable, Miracle: A Year of Food Life.* New York: Harper Perennial, 2007.

Kochhar, Rakesh. "How Americans Compare with the Global Middle Cass." Pew Research Center. July 09, 2015. Accessed February 06, 2018. http://www.pewresearch.org/ fact-tank/2015/07/09/how-americans-compare-with-the-global-middle-class/.

Kodjak, Alison. "FDA Bans 19 Chemicals Used in Antibacterial Soaps." NPR. September 02, 2016. Accessed February 07, 2018. http://www.npr.org/sections/health-shots/2016/09/02/492394717/fda-bans-19-chemicals-used-in-antibacterial-soaps.

Kolbert, Elizabeth. "Tutu, In New York, Calls for Economic Sanctions." The New York Times. January 06, 1986. Accessed March 07, 2018. http://www.nytimes. com/1986/01/07/nyregion/tutu-in-new-york-calls-for-economic-sanctions.html.

Korb, Lawrence J., and Eric Goepel. "The Case for the Draft." USnews.com. February 11, 2016. Accessed March 7, 2018. https://www.usnews.com/opinion/blogs/world-report/articles/2016–02–11/reinstate-the-draft-dont-just-expand-selective-service-to-women.

Kozakiewicz, Patrick. "The Disposal of Nuclear Waste into the World's Oceans." CBRNe Portal. January 28, 2014. Accessed March 27, 2018. https://www.cbrneportal.com/the-disposal-of-nuclear-waste-into-the-worlds-oceans/.

Krantz, Matt. "27 Giant Profitable Companies Paid No Taxes." USA Today. March 07, 2016. Accessed February 21, 2018. https://www.usatoday.com/story/money/markets/2016/03/07/27-giant-profitable-companies-paid-no-taxes/81399094/.

Kranz, Michal. "A Holocaust Denier and Former Nazi Party Leader Is Poised to ecome the Republican Nominee for Congress in Illinois." Business Insider. February 05, 2018. Accessed February 11, 2018. http://www.businessinsider.com/holocaust-denier-running-for-congress-in-illinois-2018–2.

Kujawa-Holbrook, Sheryl A. "Love and Power: Antiracist Pastoral Care.". In *Injustice and the Care of Souls: Taking Oppression Seriously in Pastoral Care*, edited by Sheryl A. Kujawa-Holbrook and Karen B. Montagno, 13–27. Minneapolis, MN: Fortress, 2009.

Laws.com. "What Was the Three Fifths Compromise?" Constitution.laws.com. Accessed February 08, 2018. https://constitution.laws.com/three-fifths-compromise.

Lawton, Geoff. "Permaculture Greening the Desert - Geoff Lawton." *YouTube*, YouTube, 25 Feb. 2015, Accessed January 18, 2018www.youtube.com/watch?v=2xcZS7arcgk.

LoBianco, Tom. "Report: Nixon's War on Drugs Targeted Black People." CNN. March 24, 2016. Accessed February 16, 2018. https://www.cnn.com/2016/03/23/politics/john-ehrlichman-richard-nixon-drug-war-blacks-hippie/index.html.

Loew, Tracy. "Roundup a 'Probable Carcinogen,' WHO Report Says." USA Today. March 20, 2015. Accessed January 18, 2018. https://www.usatoday.com/story/news/nation/2015/03/20/roundup-probable-carcinogen-report-says/25115481/.

Logsdon, Gene. *The Contrary Farmer*. White River Junction, VT: Chelsea Green, 2005.

Lutz, Amy. "Who Joins the Military: A Look at Race, Class, and Immigration Status." Syracuse University Surface. 2008. Accessed March 7, 2018. https://surface.syr.edu/cgi/viewcontent.cgi?referer=https://duckduckgo.com/&httpsredir=1&article=1002&context=soc.

Lyons, Kate. "Can We Fix It? The Repair Cafes Waging War on Throwaway Culture." The Guardian. March 15, 2018. Accessed March 27, 2018. https://www.theguardian.com/world/2018/mar/15/can-we-fix-it-the-repair-cafes-waging-war-on-throwaway-culture.

Madar, Chase. "Vietnam: A War on Civilians." The American Conservative. July 30, 2013. Accessed February 28, 2018. http://www.theamericanconservative.com/articles/vietnam-a-war-on-civilians/.

Mader, Jackie. "Back to School, but without Books and Basics in Mississippi." The Hechinger Report. August 26, 2013. Accessed February 16, 2018. http://hechingerreport.org/back-to-school-but-without-books-and-basics-in-mississippi/.

Malewitz, Jim. "Texas Voter ID Law Violates Voting Rights Act, Court Rules." The Texas Tribune. July 20, 2016. Accessed February 15, 2018. https://www.texastribune.org/2016/07/20/appeals-court-rules-texas-voter-id/.

Malone, Andrew. "The GM Genocide: Thousands of Indian Farmers Are Committing Suicide after Using Genetically Modified Crops." Daily Mail Online. November 02, 2008. Accessed January 18, 2018. http://www.dailymail.co.uk/news/article-1082559/

The-GM-genocide-Thousands-Indian-farmers-committing-suicide-using-genetically-modified-crops.html.

Mann, Charles C. *1491: New Revelations of the Americas before Columbus*. New York: Knopf, 2012.

Markova, Dawna. *The Open Mind: Discovering the 6 Patterns of Natural Intelligence*. Berkeley, CA: Conari, 1996.

Marshall, F. Ray. "The Implications of the North American Free Trade Agreement for Workers." Center for Immigration Studies. February 1, 1993. Accessed February 6, 2018. https://cis.org/Report/Implications-North-American-Free-Trade-Agreement-Workers.

Matfess, Hilary. "OPINION: US Support for Chad May Destabilize the Sahel." Al Jazeera America. March 6, 2015. Accessed March 07, 2018. http://america.aljazeera.com/opinions/2015/3/us-support-for-chad-may-destabilize-the-sahel.html.

Mathis-Lilley, Ben. "A Continually Growing List of Violent Incidents at Trump Events." Slate Magazine. April 25, 2016. Accessed February 08, 2018. http://www.slate.com/blogs/the_slatest/2016/03/02/a_list_of_violent_incidents_at_donald_trump_rallies_and_events.html.

Mazerov, Michael. "Kansas' Tax Cut Experience Refutes Economic Growth Predictions of Trump Tax Advisors." Center on Budget and Policy Priorities. October 10, 2017. Accessed February 13, 2018. https://www.cbpp.org/research/federal-tax/kansas-tax-cut-experience-refutes-economic-growth-predictions-of-trump-tax.

Mazza, Ed. "Several Eagles Players Already Planning to Skip White House Visit." The Huffington Post. February 05, 2018. Accessed February 08, 2018. https://www.huffingtonpost.com/entry/eagles-white-house-protest_us_5a78000ce4b0905433b604f2.

McCoy, Alfred W. "America and the Dictators: From Ngo Dinh Diem to Hamid Karzai." The Huffington Post. April 15, 2010. Accessed February 28, 2018. https://www.huffingtonpost.com/alfred-w-mccoy/america-and-the-dictators_b_539214.html.

McDonald, David. "The Racist Roots of Marijuana Prohibition." FEE. April 11, 2017. Accessed February 16, 2018. https://fee.org/articles/the-racist-roots-of-marijuana-prohibition/.

McKibben, Bill. *Deep Economy: The Wealth of Communities and the Durable Future*. New York, NY: Times Books, 2008.

McMickle, Marvin Andrew. *Where Have All the Prophets Gone: Reclaiming prophetic preaching in America*. Cleveland: Pilgrim, 2006.

Meadows, Donella H. *Thinking in Systems: A Primer*, edited by Diana Wright. White River Junction, VT: Chelsea Green, 2008.

Merkel, Jim. Global Living Project - Ecological Footprint. 2012. Accessed March 19, 2018. http://radicalsimplicity.org/footprint.html.

Mikkleson, David. "Hermann Goering: War Games." Snopes.com. October 4, 2002. Accessed March 09, 2018. https://www.snopes.com/fact-check/war-games/.

Milesi, C., C. D. Elvige, and J. D. Dietz. "A Strategy for Mapping and Modeling the Ecological Effects of US Lawns." ISPRS.org. Accessed February 7, 2018. http://www.isprs.org/proceedings/XXXVI/8-W27/milesi.pdf.

Millison Interview." E-mail interview by author. March 16, 2018.

Modern Farmer. "12 Fantastic Victory Garden Posters." Modern Farmer. May 13, 2013. Accessed February 07, 2018. http://modernfarmer.com/2013/05/12-fantastic-victory-garden-posters/.

Mollison, Bill. *Permaculture: A Designer's Manual*, edited by Reny Mia Slay. 2nd ed. Tyalgum, AU: Tagari Publications, 2009.

———. *Permaculture: A Designer's Manual*. Tasmania: Tagari, 1988.

Montgomery, David R. *Dirt: The Erosion of Civilizations*. Berkeley, CA: University of California Press, 2012.

Mosher, Dave. "Trump Wants to Make Nuclear Weapons Easier to Use - and His Plan Is a Roadmap for Nuclear War." Business Insider. January 17, 2018. Accessed March 07, 2018. http://www.businessinsider.com/nuclear-posture-review-trump-huffpost-draft-report-2018–1.

Mui, Ylan Q. "For Black Americans, Financial Damage from Subprime Implosion Is Likely to Last." The Washington Post. July 08, 2012. Accessed February 16, 2018. https://www.washingtonpost.com/business/economy/for-black-americans-financial-damage-from-subprime-implosion-is-likely-to-last/2012/07/08/gJQAwNmzWW_story.html?utm_term=.8dd1378910e7.

NASA. "Global Climate Change: Effects." August 03, 2017. Accessed February 01, 2018. https://climate.nasa.gov/effects/.

———. "Scientific Consensus: Earth's Climate is Warming." October 18, 2017. Accessed January 06, 2018. https://climate.nasa.gov/scientific-consensus/.

National Academy of Sciences. "Where is the Earth's Water?" Safe Drinking Water is Essential. September 01, 2007. Accessed February 07, 2018. https://www.koshland-science-museum.org/water/html/en/Sources/Where-is-the-Earths-Water.html.

National Capital Poison Center. "Poison Statistics National Data 2016." Poison Control: National Capital Poison Center. Accessed February 07, 2018. http://www.poison.org/poison-statistics-national.

National Center for Biotechnology Information. "Human and Environmental Toxicity of Sodium Lauryl Sulfate (SLS): Evidence for Safe Use in Household Cleaning Products." National Center for Biotechnology Information. November 17, 2015. Accessed February 7, 2018. https://www.ncbi.nlm.nih.gov/pmc/articles/PMC4651417/.

Nebehay, Stephanie. "U.N. Says 300 Civilians Killed in U.S.-Led Airstrikes in Raqqa" Reuters. June 14, 2017. Accessed February 28, 2018. https://www.reuters.com/article/us-mideast-crisis-syria-warcrimes/u-n-says-300-civilians-killed-in-u-s-led-air-strikes-in-raqqa-since-march-idUSKBN19511O.

Nesbit, Jeff. "America, Racial Bias Does Exist." U.S. News & World Report. January 13, 2015. Accessed February 13, 2018. https://www.usnews.com/news/blogs/at-the-edge/2015/01/13/america-racial-bias-does-exist.

New York Civil Liberties Union "Stop-and-Frisk Data." July 29, 2017. Accessed February 16, 2018. https://www.nyclu.org/en/stop-and-frisk-data.

The New York Times. "Bee Survival in Europe." October 26, 2013. Accessed March 19, 2018. http://www.nytimes.com/2013/10/26/opinion/international/bee-survival-in-europe.html.

———. "Unequal Sentences for Blacks and Whites." December 17, 2016. Accessed February 16, 2018. https://www.nytimes.com/2016/12/17/opinion/sunday/unequal-sentences-for-blacks-and-whites.html.

NOAA Office of Response and Restoration "How Big Is the 'Great Pacific Garbage Patch'"? Science vs. Myth.". February 7, 2013. Accessed February 06, 2018. https://response.restoration.noaa.gov/about/media/how-big-great-pacific-garbage-patch-science-vs-myth.html.

NOAA. "Description of the Hydrologic Cycle." Northwest River Forecast Center (NWRFC) web site. October 22, 2002. Accessed February 07, 2018. https://www.nwrfc.noaa.gov/info/water_cycle/hydrology.cgi.

Norton, Ben. "Bill Clinton Continues to Defend 1994 Crime Bill That Fueled Racist Mass Incarceration." Salon. May 14, 2016. Accessed February 16, 2018. https://www.salon.com/2016/05/13/bill_clinton_continues_to_defend_1994_crime_bill_that_fueled_racist_mass_incarceration/.

———."Un-Democratic Party: DNC Chair Says Superdelegates Ensure Elites Don't Have to Run 'Against Grassroots Activists'" Salon. February 13, 2016. Accessed February 11, 2018. https://www.salon.com/2016/02/13/un_democratic_party_dnc_chair_says_superdelegates_ensure_elites_dont_have_to_run_against_grassroots_activists/.

NRCS, New Hampshire. "How to Read a Topographic Map and Delineate a Watershed." USDA National Resource Conservation Service. Accessed March 27, 2018. https://www.nrcs.usda.gov/Internet/FSE_DOCUMENTS/nrcs144p2_014819.pdf.

O'Connor, Clare. "Report: Walmart Workers Cost Taxpayers $6.2 Billion In Public Assistance." Forbes. April 16, 2014. Accessed February 16, 2018. https://www.forbes.com/sites/clareoconnor/2014/04/15/report-walmart-workers-cost-taxpayers-6-2-billion-in-public-assistance/#177f458f720b.

Onion, Rebecca. "Take the Impossible 'Literacy' Test Louisiana Gave Black Voters in the 1960s." Slate Magazine. June 28, 2013. Accessed February 08, 2018. http://www.slate.com/blogs/the_vault/2013/06/28/voting_rights_and_the_supreme_court_the_impossible_literacy_test_louisiana.html.

Organic Consumers Association. "How Toxic Are Your Bathroom and Your Body Care Products." October 25, 2005. Accessed February 07, 2018. https://www.organicconsumers.org/old_articles/bodycare/bathroom102605.php.

———."How Toxic Are Your Household Cleaning Supplies?" Accessed February 07, 2018. https://www.organicconsumers.org/news/how-toxic-are-your-household-cleaning-supplies.

Ovalle, David, and Sarah Blaskey. "Parkland School Shooter Nikolas Cruz Makes First Live Appearance in Court." MSN.com. February 20, 2018. Accessed March 07, 2018. https://www.msn.com/en-us/news/us/parkland-school-shooter-nikolas-cruz-makes-first-live-appearance-in-court/ar-BBJltqP.

Ozeki, Ruth L. All Over Creation. London: Picador, 2004.

———. My Year of Meats. New York: Penguin, 1999.

PBS. "Napalm and The Dow Chemical Company." Accessed March 01, 2018. http://www.pbs.org/wgbh/americanexperience/features/two-days-in-october-dow-chemical-and-use-napalm/.

Palermo, Elizabeth. "Do Indoor Plants Really Clean the Air?" LiveScience. July 29, 2013. Accessed February 7, 2018. http://www.livescience.com/38445-indoor-plants-clean-air.html.

Palmer, Brian. "Landfills: Are We Running out of Room for Our Garbage?" Slate Magazine. February 15, 2011. Accessed February 06, 2018. http://www.slate.com/articles/health_and_science/the_green_lantern/2011/02/go_west_garbage_can.html.

Parker, Kim, Anthony Cilluffo, and Renee Stepler. "6 Facts about the U.S. Military and Its Changing Demographics." Pew Research Center. April 13, 2017. Accessed March 07, 2018. http://www.pewresearch.org/fact-tank/2017/04/13/6-facts-about-the-u-s-military-and-its-changing-demographics/.

Patton, Mike. "The Facts on Increasing the Minimum Wage." Forbes. April 13, 2016. Accessed February 16, 2018. https://www.forbes.com/sites/mikepatton/2014/11/26/the-facts-on-the-minimum-wage-increase/#2cb9b3f133a1.

Perkins, John. *Confessions of an Economic Hitman.* San Francisco: Berret-Koehler, 2004.

Perlman, Howard. "What is a Watershed? Watersheds and Drainage Basins." USGS Water Science School. December 9, 2016. Accessed January 18, 2018. https://water.usgs.gov/edu/watershed.html.

Perry, Brian. "4 Key Indicators That Move the Markets." Investopedia. November 15, 2017. Accessed February 06, 2018. http://www.investopedia.com/articles/fundamental-analysis/10/indicators-that-move-the-market.asp.

Philpott, Tom. "Many Meat Producers Claim Their Operations Don't Produce Superbugs. The US Government Begs to Differ." Mother Jones. June 24, 2017. Accessed July 27, 2017. http://www.motherjones.com/tom-philpott/2013/09/cdc-meat-industry-yes-you-contribute-antibiotic-resistance/.

Pierce, Jane. "Nonpoint Source Pollution Education: Fertilizing the Lawn | MassDEP." Mass.gov: Energy and Environmental Affairs. November 13, 2012. Accessed February 07, 2018. http://www.mass.gov/eea/agencies/massdep/water/watersheds/fertilizing-the-lawn.html.

Pike, John. "Military Personnel." Accessed March 07, 2018. https://www.globalsecurity.org/military/agency/end-strength.htm.

Pilger, John. "Friends of Pol Pot." Global Policy Forum. May 1, 1998. Accessed February 28, 2018. https://www.globalpolicy.org/component/content/article/190/39190.html.

Pokharel, Sugam. "Why India's Cotton Farmers are Killing Themselves." CNN. April 20, 2015. Accessed January 18, 2018. http://www.cnn.com/2015/04/19/asia/india-cotton-farmers-suicide/index.html.

Potok, Mark. "The Year in Hate and Extremism." Southern Poverty Law Center. February 15, 2017. Accessed February 08, 2018. https://www.splcenter.org/fighting-hate/intelligence-report/2017/year-hate-and-extremism.

Poultry Hub. "Beak Trimming." Accessed July 12, 2017. http://www.poultryhub.org/health/health-management/beak-trimming/.

Precious Plastic. "Precious Plastic." Accessed March 27, 2018. https://preciousplastic.com/.

Proulx, Annie. *That Old Ace in the Hole.* New York: Scribner, 2002.

Rabinovitch, Ari, Michelle Nichols, and Tom Perry. "Israel Imposes 'Apartheid Regime' on Palestinians: U.N. Report." Reuters. March 16, 2017. Accessed March 07, 2018. https://www.reuters.com/article/us-israel-palestinians-report/israel-imposes-apartheid-regime-on-palestinians-u-n-report-idUSKBN16M2IN.

Rapoza, Kenneth. "Fox News Viewers Uninformed, NPR Listeners Not, Poll Suggests." Forbes. July 15, 2016. Accessed March 07, 2018. https://www.forbes.com/sites/kenrapoza/2011/11/21/fox-news-viewers-uninformed-npr-listeners-not-poll-suggests/#7f9a52bc4fd8.

Reilly, P.J. "How Sick is the Susquehanna?" Lancaster Online. October 28, 2012. Accessed January 18, 2018. http://lancasteronline.com/sports/how-sick-is-the-susquehanna-river/article_b4155adb-9c5c-575a-95c6-948c53b276b1.html .

Renegade, Gus T. "No, Thomas Jefferson and Sally Hemings Did Not Have a Relationship." Atlanta Black Star. February 25, 2017. Accessed February 15, 2018. http://atlantablackstar.com/2017/02/25/no-thomas-jefferson-sally-hemings-not-relationship/.

Responsible Purchasing Network "Cleaners: Social & Environmental." Accessed February 07, 2018. http://www.responsiblepurchasing.org/purchasing_guides/cleaners/social_environ/.

Rhoades, Heather. "What Are Nitrogen Fixing Plants." Gardening Know How. November 27, 2016. Accessed February 07, 2018. https://www.gardeningknowhow.com/garden-how-to/soil-fertilizers/nitrogen-nodules-and-nitrogen-fixing-plants.htm.

Ridley, Yvonne. "Bush Convicted of War Crimes in Absentia." Foreign Policy Journal. May 12, 2012. Accessed February 6, 2018. https://www.foreignpolicyjournal.com/2012/05/12/bush-convicted-of-war-crimes-in-absentia/.

Rifai, Ryan. "Polls: Sanders Has More Potential to Beat Trump." US & Canada | Al Jazeera. May 14, 2016. Accessed February 11, 2018. https://www.aljazeera.com/indepth/features/2016/05/polls-sanders-potential-beat-trump-160514170035436.html.

Riley, Katie. "What to Know about Recent Immigration Raids in U.S. Cities." Fortune. February 11, 2017. Accessed February 11, 2018. http://fortune.com/2017/02/11/immigration-raids-us-cities/.

Risen, Tim. "Scientist Warn Congress Not to Ignore Climate Change." U.S. News and World Report. June 28, 2016. Accessed February 1, 2018. https://www.usnews.com/news/articles/2016–06–28/scientists-warn-congress-not-to-ignore-climate-change.

Rodale Institute. "The Farming Systems Trial: Celebrating 30 Years." Accessed January 18, 2018. http://rodaleinstitute.org/assets/FSTbookletFINAL.pdf.

RT International. "Obama Unapologetic over US Support of Pinochet." March 22, 2011. Accessed February 28, 2018. https://www.rt.com/usa/obama-unapologetic-usa-chile-pinochet/.

Ruether, Rosemary Radford. *Gaia & God: An Ecofeminist Theology of Earth Healing.* New York, NY: Harper, 1992.

Rushe, Dominic. "Kansas's Ravaged Economy a Cautionary Tale as Trump Plans Huge Tax Cuts for Rich." The Guardian. December 10, 2017. Accessed February 13, 2018. https://www.theguardian.com/us-news/2017/dec/10/donald-trump-kansas-failed-tax-cuts.

SOA Watch: "Notorious Graduates." April 10, 2012. Accessed March 09, 2018. http://soaw.org/about-the-soawhinsec/soawhinsec-grads/notorious-grads.

Sachs, Jeffrey D. "The Fatal Expense of American Imperialism - The Boston Globe." BostonGlobe.com. October 30, 2016. Accessed February 06, 2018. https://www.bostonglobe.com/opinion/2016/10/30/the-fatal-expense-american-imperialism/teXS2xwA1UJbYd1oWJBHHM/story.html.

Saletan, William. "Ted Cruz's Shameful Attempts to Blur the Line between Muslims and Islamic Extremists." Slate Magazine. December 11, 2015. Accessed February 08, 2018. http://www.slate.com/articles/news_and_politics/politics/2015/12/ted_cruz_s_latest_anti_muslim_rhetoric_is_beyond_shameful.html.

Samenow, Jason. "North Pole Surges above Freezing in the Dead of Winter, Stunning Scientists." The Washington Post. February 26, 2018. Accessed March 28, 2018. https://www.washingtonpost.com/news/capital-weather-gang/wp/2018/02/26/north-pole-surges-above-freezing-in-the-dead-of-winter-stunning-scientists/?utm_term=.8fc07ad738a2.

Savory, Allan. "Savory Institute." Savory Institute. Accessed January 18, 2018. http://www.savory.global/institute/.

Schaefer, Anna. "7 Ways Dandelion Tea Could Be Good for You." Healthline. Accessed March 27, 2018. https://www.healthline.com/health/ways-dandelion-tea-could-be-good-for-your#1.

Schilgden, Bob. "Hey Mr. Green, Can You Compost Shredded Paper?" Sierra Club. March 25, 2015. Accessed February 06, 2018. https://www.sierraclub.org/sierra/2013-2-march-april/green-life/hey-mr-green-can-you-compost-shredded-paper.

Schlesinger, Stephen C., Stephen Kinzer, and John H. Coatsworth. *Bitter Fruit: The Story of the American coup in Guatemala.* Cambridge, MA: Harvard University, David Rockefeller Center for Latin American Studies, 2005.

Schlosser, Eric. *Fast Food Nation: What the All-American Meal is Doing to the World.* London: Penguin, 2002.

Schottey, Michael. "The Flag and the Shield: The Long Alliance Between the NFL and US Military." Bleacher Report. April 09, 2017. Accessed March 09, 2018. http://bleacherreport.com/articles/2029052-the-flag-and-the-shield-the-long-alliance-between-the-nfl-and-the-us-military.

Science Daily. "Toxic Chemicals Found in Common Scented Laundry Products." ScienceDaily. July 24, 2008. Accessed February 07, 2018. https://www.sciencedaily.com/releases/2008/07/080723134438.htm.

Scientific American. "How Fertilizers Harm Earth More than Help Your Lawn." Scientific American. Accessed February 07, 2018. https://www.scientificamerican.com/article/how-fertilizers-harm-earth/.

Scott, Robert E. "Free Trade in the Americas: Labor and Environmental Concerns." Economic Policy Institute. April 29, 1998. Accessed February 06, 2018. http://www.epi.org/publication/free-trade-americas-labor-environmental/.

———."The High Price of 'Free' Trade: NAFTA's Failure Has Cost the United States Jobs across the Nation." Economic Policy Institute. November 17, 2003. Accessed February 06, 2018. http://www.epi.org/publication/briefingpapers_bp147/.

Scribol. "20 Brutal Dictators Supported by the U.S. - Page 10 of 21." Scribol.com. September 18, 2015. Accessed February 28, 2018. http://scribol.com/anthropology-and-history/people/brutal-dictators-supported-by-united-states/10/.

Seidule, Ty. "Was the Civil War About Slavery?" YouTube. August 10, 2015. Accessed

Selk, Avi. "Gun Owners Are Outraged by the Philando Castile Case. The NRA Is Silent." The Washington Post. June 21, 2017. Accessed February 16, 2018. https://www.washingtonpost.com/news/post-nation/wp/2017/06/18/some-gun-owners-are-disturbed-by-the-philando-castile-verdict-the-nra-is-silent/?utm_term=.031a70b1b082.

Shah, Anup. "Poverty Facts and Stats." Global Issues. January 7, 2013. Accessed February 06, 2018. http://www.globalissues.org/article/26/poverty-facts-and-stats.

Sierra Club. "Why are CAFOs Bad?" December 04, 2017. Accessed January 18, 2018. http://www.sierraclub.org/michigan/why-are-cafos-bad.

Simmons, Tony. "Locate, Close with and Destroy." The Official United States Marine Corps Public Website. January 20, 2015. Accessed March 07, 2018. http://www.marines.mil/News/News-Display/Article/560453/locate-close-with-and-destroy/.

"Sinful Sermon?" Sermon of Salvation from Savages. Accessed February 15, 2018. http://home.nwciowa.edu/lundberg/SEssays/rhetoric/response2.htm.

Snider, Laura. "Gas Lawn Mowers Belch Pollution." Boulder Daily Camera. July 27, 2007. Accessed February 07, 2018. http://www.dailycamera.com/ci_13084336.

Spetalnick, Matt. "U.S. Lifted Uzbekistan's Rights Ranking as Cotton Field Abuses..." Reuters. December 23, 2015. Accessed March 07, 2018. https://www.reuters.com/ article/us-usa-humantrafficking-uzbekistan-insig/u-s-lifted-uzbekistans-rights-ranking-as-cotton-field-abuses-continued-idUSKBN0U60EZ20151223.

Stamets, Paul. *Mycelium Running: How Mushrooms Can Help Save the World.* Berkeley: Ten Speed Press, 2005.

Steele, Dylan. "Cleaner Air: Gas Mower Pollution Facts." Cleaner Air: Mowing Emissions and Clean Air Alternatives. A Fact Sheet. Accessed February 07, 2018. https://www. peoplepoweredmachines.com/faq-environment.htm.

Stein, Rob. "New Nixon Tapes Reveal Anti-Semitic, Racist Remarks." The Washington Post. December 12, 2010. Accessed February 16, 2018. http://www.washingtonpost. com/wp-dyn/content/article/2010/12/11/AR2010121102890.html.

Strom, Stephanie. "A Sweetheart Becomes Suspect; Looking Behind Those Kathie Lee Labels." The New York Times. June 26, 1996. Accessed February 06, 2018. http:// www.nytimes.com/1996/06/27/business/a-sweetheart-becomes-suspect-looking-behind-those-kathie-lee-labels.html.

Stuart, Tessa. "1.15 Million Americans Killed by Guns Since John Lennon." Rolling Stone. December 08, 2015. Accessed February 08, 2018. https://www.rollingstone. com/politics/news/1–15-million-americans-have-been-killed-by-guns-since-john-lennons-death-20151208.

Tang, Eric. "'A Society Gone Mad on War: The Enduring Importance of Martin Luther King's Riverside Speech." The Nation. April 05, 2017. Accessed March 09, 2018. https://www.thenation.com/article/a-society-gone-mad-on-war-the-enduring-importance-of-martin-luther-kings-riverside-speech/.

Taylor, Adam, and Laris Karklis. "This Remarkable Chart Shows How U.S. Defense Spending Dwarfs the Rest of the World." The Washington Post. February 09, 2016. Accessed March 01, 2018. https://www.washingtonpost.com/news/worldviews/ wp/2016/02/09/this-remarkable-chart-shows-how-u-s-defense-spending-dwarfs-the-rest-of-the-world/?utm_term=.60caac8c4e08.

teleSUR English "Haitian Workers Fight for Higher Minimum Wage Suppressed by Clinton's State Department." May 22, 2017. Accessed February 06, 2018. https:// www.telesurtv.net/english/news/Haitians-Workers-Fight-for-Higher-Minimum-Wage-Suppressed-by-Clintons-State-Department-20170522–0037.html.

Tharoor, Ishaan. "Analysis | Trumps Saber-Rattling at North Korea Sparks Fears and Puts China in a Bind." The Washington Post. August 10, 2017. Accessed February 11, 2018. https://www.washingtonpost.com/news/worldviews/wp/2017/08/10/trumps-saber-rattling-at-north-korea-sparks-fears-and-puts-china-in-a-bind/?utm_term=. d13134ce55de.

Thayer, Robert L. *LifePlace: Bioregional Thought and Practice.* Berkeley: University of California Press, 2003.

Thayer, Samuel. "Our Books." Foragers Harvest. Accessed February 07, 2018. http://www. foragersharvest.com/our-books.html.

Tirman, John. "Why Do We Ignore the Civilians Killed in American Wars?" The Washington Post. January 06, 2012. Accessed March 07, 2018. https://www.washingtonpost.com/ opinions/why-do-we-ignore-the-civilians-killed-in-american-wars/2011/12/05/ gIQALCO4eP_story.html?utm_term=.a3fdb2a64b5a.

Toensmeier, Eric. "Paradise Lot: Two Plant Geeks, One Tenth of an Acre, and the Making of an Edible Garden Oasis in the City." PerennialSolutions.org. November 13, 2017.

Accessed February 07, 2018. http://www.perennialsolutions.org/paradise-lot-two-plant-geeks-one-tenth-of-an-acre-and-the-making-of-an-edible-garden-oasis-in-the-city.

Turner, Cory, Reema Khrais, and Tim Lloyd. "Why America's Schools Have A Money Problem." NPR. April 18, 2016. Accessed February 16, 2018. https://www.npr.org/2016/04/18/474256366/why-americas-schools-have-a-money-problem.

Turse, Nick. "Why Is the US Military So Interested in Chad?" The Nation. June 29, 2015. Accessed March 07, 2018. https://www.thenation.com/article/why-us-military-so-interested-chad/.

Tutton, Mark. "40 Million Slaves in The World, Finds New Report." CNN. September 20, 2017. Accessed February 06, 2018. https://www.cnn.com/2017/09/19/world/global-slavery-estimates-ilo/index.html.

U.S. Department of Commerce, National Oceanic and Atmospheric Administration. "What is a Dead Zone?" NOAA's National Ocean Service. August 01, 2014. Accessed January 18, 2018. https://oceanservice.noaa.gov/facts/deadzone.html.

U.S. Department of Defense. "Department of Defense (DoD) Releases Fiscal Year 2017 President's Budget." February 9, 2016. Accessed March 07, 2018. https://www.defense.gov/News/News-Releases/News-Release-View/Article/652687/department-of-defense-dod-releases-fiscal-year-2017-presidents-budget-proposal/.

U.S. Food and Drug Administration. "Bovine Somatotropin (BST)." October 27, 2017. Accessed January 18, 2018. https://www.fda.gov/AnimalVeterinary/SafetyHealth/ProductSafetyInformation/ucm055435.html.

———. "Web Soil Survey." Accessed March 27, 2018. https://websoilsurvey.sc.egov.usda.gov/App/WebSoilSurvey.aspx.

UNCTAD. "Wake up Before it Is Too Late: Make Agriculture Truly Sustainable Now for Food Security in a Changing Climate." September 18, 2013. Accessed January 18, 2018. http://unctad.org/en/PublicationsLibrary/ditcted2012d3_en.pdf.

Union of Concerned Scientists "How Do We Know that Humans Are the Major Cause of Global Warming?". August 1, 2017. Accessed March 01, 2018. https://www.ucsusa.org/global-warming/science-and-impacts/science/human-contribution-to-gw-faq.html#bf-toc-1.

United Nations. "Water." Accessed February 07, 2018. http://www.un.org/en/sections/issues-depth/water/index.html.

United States Environmental Protection Agency. "The City of Lancaster, PA Clean Water Act Settlement." EPA. January 04, 2018. Accessed March 19, 2018. https://www.epa.gov/enforcement/city-lancaster-pa-clean-water-act-settlement.

University of Utah. "How Much Do Americans Throw Away." Accessed February 6, 2018. http://students.arch.utah.edu/courses/Arch4011/Recycling%20Facts1.pdf.

Valentine, Matt, and Thich Nhat Hanh. "101 Inspiring Mindfulness Quotes to Live By." Buddhaimonia. 2017. Accessed March 21, 2018. https://buddhaimonia.com/blog/101-mindfulness-quotes.

van Tets, Fernande. "Exodus: Terrified Syrians Dash to Flee Air Strikes." The Independent. August 31, 2013. Accessed March 09, 2018. http://www.independent.co.uk/news/world/middle-east/exodus-terrified-syrians-dash-to-flee-air-strikes-8792973.html.

"Versions of the Golden Rule in Dozens of Religions and Other Sources." Accessed June 8, 2017. http://www.religioustolerance.org/reciproc2.htm.

Veterans of the Civil Rights Movement. "Voting Rights Are You 'Qualified' to Vote? Take a 'Literacy Test' to Find Out". Accessed February 08, 2018. http://www.crmvet.org/info/lithome.htm.

Vidal, John. "The 7,000km Journey That Links Amazon Destruction to Fast Food." The Guardian. April 06, 2006. Accessed March 27, 2018. https://www.theguardian.com/business/2006/apr/06/brazil.food.

Volf, Miroslav. *Flourishing: Why We Need Religion in a Globalized World*. New Haven, CT: Yale University Press, 2017.

Walters, Jonah. "'Just Cause' and Its Aftermath." Jacobin. Accessed March 07, 2018. https://jacobinmag.com/2017/05/panama-noriega-operation-just-cause-reagan-imperialism.

Ward, Scott. "There Is No Way to Peace, Peace Is the Way": A.J. Muste and American Radical Pacifism | Origins: Current Events in Historical Perspective. February 2015. Accessed March 09, 2018. http://origins.osu.edu/review/there-no-way-peace-peace-way-aj-muste-and-american-radical-pacifism.

Weaver, J. Denny. *The Nonviolent Atonement*. Grand Rapids, MI: William B. Eerdmans, 2011.

The Week." 5 Dictators the U.S. Still Supports." February 03, 2011. Accessed February 28, 2018. https://theweek.com/articles/487538/5-dictators-still-supports.

The Week. "Blades of Glory: America's Love Affair with the Lawn." The Week. Accessed February 7, 2018. http://theweek.com/articles/483762/blades-glory-americas-love-affair-lawns .

Wernick, Adam. "IMF: 'True cost' of Fossil Fuels is $5.3 Trillion a Year." Public Radio International. June 7, 2015. Accessed February 06, 2018. https://www.pri.org/stories/2015–06–07/imf-true-cost-fossil-fuels-53-trillion-year.

Westervelt, Amy. "Chemical Enemy Number One: How Bad Are Phthalates Really?" The Guardian. February 10, 2015. Accessed February 07, 2018. https://www.theguardian.com/lifeandstyle/2015/feb/10/phthalates-plastics-chemicals-research-analysis.

The White House. "Press Briefing by Ari Fleischer." National Archives and Records Administration. May 7, 2001. Accessed March 23, 2018. https://georgewbush-whitehouse.archives.gov/news/briefings/20010507.html.

Whitney, Rich. "US Provides Military Assistance to 73 Percent of World's Dictatorships." Medium. September 23, 2017. Accessed February 28, 2018. https://medium.com/@richwhitney/us-provides-military-assistance-to-73-percent-of-worlds-dictatorships-d679770415cc.

Wile, Rob. "The American Lawn Is Now the Largest Single Crop in The U.S." The Huffington Post. August 17, 2015. Accessed February 07, 2018. http://www.huffingtonpost.com/entry/lawn-largest-crop-america_us_55d0dc06e4b07addcb43435d.

Williams, Timothy. "Marijuana Arrests Outnumber Those for Violent Crimes, Study Finds." The New York Times. October 12, 2016. Accessed February 16, 2018. https://www.nytimes.com/2016/10/13/us/marijuana-arrests.html.

Williams, Vanessa. "Democrats Say Alabama's Closure of Drivers-License Offices Could Make It Harder for Black Residents To Vote." The Washington Post. October 02, 2015. Accessed February 13, 2018. https://www.washingtonpost.com/news/post-politics/wp/2015/10/02/democrats-say-alabamas-closure-of-drivers-license-offices-could-make-it-harder-for-black-residents-to-vote/?utm_term=.0f8735b1c02a.

Wilson, Lydia. "What I Discovered from Interviewing Imprisoned ISIS Fighters." The Nation. March 22, 2016. Accessed March 09, 2018. https://www.thenation.com/article/what-i-discovered-from-interviewing-isis-prisoners/.

Wilson, Taylor. "Consumer Spending on Household Cleaning Supplies." E-mail message to author. February 9, 2018.

Wink, Walter. *Engaging the Powers: Discernment and resistance in a world of domination.* Minneapolis, MN: Fortress, 1992.

———. *Naming the Powers: The Language of Power in the New Testament.* Philadelphia: Fortress, 1984.

———. *Unmasking the Powers - The Invisible Forces That Determine Human Existence.* Philadelphia: Fortress, 1986.

Wolcott, Ben. "2014 Job Creation Faster in States that Raised the Minimum Wage." CEPR. June 30, 2014. Accessed February 16, 2018. http://cepr.net/blogs/cepr-blog/2014-job-creation-in-states-that-raised-the-minimum-wage.

Worland, Justin. "Scott Pruitt's Mission to Remake the EPA." Time. October 26, 2017. Accessed February 08, 2018. http://time.com/4998279/company-man-in-washington/.

World Forum on Natural Capital. "What Is Natural Capital?" 2017. Accessed March 27, 2018. https://naturalcapitalforum.com/about/.

Yablon, Alex, and Mike Spies. "The NRA Has Already Spent More Money on Lobbying in 2017 Than It Did All Last Year." Business Insider. September 12, 2017. Accessed February 16, 2018. http://www.businessinsider.com/nra-spending-budget-lobbying-in-2017-2017-9.

Yeomans, Ken B., and P. A. Yeomans. *Water for Every Farm: Yeomans Keyline Plan.* Southport, Qld.: Keyline Designs, 2008.

Zahnd, Brian. *A Farewell to Mars: An Evangelical Pastor's Journey toward the Biblical Gospel of Peace.* Colorado Springs, CO: David C Cook, 2014.

Zarroli, Jim. "In Trendy World of Fast Fashion, Styles Aren't Made to Last." NPR. March 11, 2013. Accessed February 06, 2018. http://www.npr.org/2013/03/11/174013774/in-trendy-world-of-fast-fashion-styles-arent-made-to-last.

Zinn, Howard, and Anthony Arnove. *A People's History of the United States.* Modern Classics ed. New York: Harper Perennial, 2015.